Lecture Notes in Artificial Intelligence   770

Subseries of Lecture Notes in Computer Science
Edited by J. G. Carbonell and J. Siekmann

Lecture Notes in Computer Science

Edited by G. Goos and J. Hartmanis

Lecture Notes in Artificial Intelligence 770

Subseries of Lecture Notes in Computer Science
Edited by J. G. Carbonell and J. Siekmann

Lecture Notes in Computer Science
Edited by G. Goos and J. Hartmanis

Peter Haddawy

Representing Plans Under Uncertainty

A Logic of Time, Chance, and Action

Springer-Verlag
Berlin Heidelberg NewYork
London Paris Tokyo
Hong Kong Barcelona
Budapest

Series Editors

Jaime G. Carbonell
School of Computer Science, Carnegie Mellon University
Schenley Park, Pittsburgh, PA 15213-3890, USA

Jörg Siekmann
University of Saarland
German Research Center for Artificial Intelligence (DFKI)
Stuhlsatzenhausweg 3, D-66123 Saarbrücken, Germany

Author

Peter Haddawy
Department of Electrical Engineering and Computer Science
University of Wisconsin-Milwaukee
P. O. Box 784, Milwaukee, WI 53201, USA

CR Subject Classification (1991): I.2.3, I.2.4, I.2.8

ISBN 3-540-57697-5 Springer-Verlag Berlin Heidelberg New York
ISBN 0-387-57697-5 Springer-Verlag New York Berlin Heidelberg

CIP data applied for

© Springer-Verlag Berlin Heidelberg 1994
Printed in Germany

Typesetting: Camera ready by author
SPIN: 10131023   45/3140-543210 - Printed on acid-free paper

Preface

Traditional AI planning representations have lacked explicit representation of both time and uncertainty. This lack of expressiveness has limited the applicability of traditional AI planning systems to only severly restricted domains. In order to address more realistic planning problems, researchers have turned to temporal logics. But the temporally enriched planning representations still lack the ability to represent uncertainty, as well as lacking any kind of link to a theory of rational behavior. Decision Theory provides a normative model of choice under uncertainty such that recommended choices can be said to be rational under a well-defined notion of rationality. But traditional decision-theoretic representations are limited in their ability to structure knowledge other than beliefs and preferences.

This monograph integrates AI and decision-theoretic approaches to the representation of planning problems by developing a first-order logic of time, chance, and action for representing and reasoning about plans. The semantics of the logic incorporates intuitive properties of time, chance, and action central to the planning problem. The logical language integrates both modal and probabilistic constructs and allows quantification over time points, probability values, and domain individuals. Probability is treated as a sentential operator in the language, so it can be arbitrarily nested and combined with other logical operators. The language can represent the chance that facts hold and events occur at various times. It can represent the chance that actions and other events affect the future. The model of action distinguishes between action feasibility, executability, and effects. Using this distinction, a notion of expected utility for acts that may not be feasible is defined. This notion is used to reason about the chance that trying a plan will achieve a given goal. An algorithm for the problem of building construction planning is developed and the logic is used to prove the algorithm correct.

Acknowledgements This monograph is a slightly revised version of my PhD dissertation, completed in August 1991 at the Department of Computer Science of the University of Illinois at Urbana-Champaign. I thank the Department of Computer Science for providing me with the computing facilities necessary to carry out this work.

My thesis benefited from the generous help of many people along the way. First I would like to thank my advisor, Alan Frisch. He was everything an advisor should be. He was always generous with both his time and his ideas. His keen sense of mathematical aesthetic and his great enthusiasm for research were sources of inspiration and motivation.

I would like to thank the other members of my committee: Patrick Maher, Marianne Winslett, George Monahan, and Caroline Hayes for their insightful comments. In particular, Patrick Maher acted as my advisor in all things decision-theoretic. I would like to thank him for introducing me to Bayesian Decision Theory and for guiding me through its subtleties. He was always ready to listen carefully and share with me his superb expertise.

Many people contributed to the development of the ideas presented in this thesis. Joe Halpern was instrumental in refining many of the ideas in my early work on probability logic. In particular, I would like to thank him for encouraging me to find an intuitive semantics for my logic. All my knowledge of the construction planning domain came from discussions with Diego Echeverry. Steve Hanks worked with me in developing the ideas relating goals to utilities. Thanks to Mike Wellman for helpful comments on some of that work.

I would like to thank the members of the Knowledge Representation and Reasoning group, Rich Scherl, David Page, and Tomas Uribe, for many helpful discussions and for providing a supportive research environment. Thanks to my officemates Scott Bennett and Dennis Decoste for generously donating their time and expertise to keep the lab running.

The research reported in this monograph was partially supported by a University of Illinois Cognitive Science/Artificial Intelligence Fellowship and a Shell Doctoral Dissertation Fellowship. The revision of the monograph was supported in part by the National Science Foundation under grant IRI–9207262.

December 1993   Peter Haddawy

Table of Contents

List of Figures

1 Introduction

Planning, the process of formulating and choosing a set of actions which when executed will likely achieve a desirable outcome, is a basic component of intelligent behavior. Actions in a plan may be performed to affect the state of knowledge of the performing agent, to affect the state of the world, or simply for their own sake. The present work focuses on the last two types of action. To choose appropriate courses of such action, an agent must reason about the state of the world, conditions in the world that his actions can influence and the extent to which he can influence them, and conversely conditions in the world that influence his actions and the extent of that influence.

Many aspects of the world are inherently stochastic, so a representation for reasoning about plans must be able to express chances of conditions in the world as well as indeterminacy in the effects of actions and events. For example, smoking does not deterministically cause lung cancer; it only greatly increases one's chance of contracting lung cancer. Uncertain environmental factors can influence a smoker's chance of contracting cancer as can uncertainty in the effects of smoking.

Reasoning about plans requires the ability to reason about time. Facts tend to be true for periods of time, and actions and events occur at particular times. Actions comprising a plan may occur sequentially or concurrently. Actions and events affect the future, but not the past. Chance evolves with time: the chance of rain tomorrow may not be the same now as it will be tonight. Ambiguities in the world are resolved with time: before a fair coin is flipped the chance of heads is 50% but after it is flipped it either certainly landed heads or it certainly did not.

This monograph presents a first-order logic of time, chance, and action for representing and reasoning about plans. The developed logic can represent all the aspects of time, chance, and action discussed above. We start by making explicit and precise commonsense notions about time, chance, and action. We then construct a logic that embodies these commonsense notions. And finally we apply that logic to the representation of planning problems. We show that by integrating the representation of both time and chance in a single framework, we can represent aspects of planning problems that cannot be represented if the two are treated separately. So through the integration we obtain a language that is more expressive than the mere sum of its parts.

The developed logic represents time in terms of possible world-histories. A world-history is a complete history of the world throughout time. Possibility is represented in terms Kripke structures [40] by defining an accessibility relation over the world-histories. Chance is represented by defining generalized Kripke structures in terms of probability distributions over the world-histories. By integrating both modal and probabilistic constructs, the logical language can represent and distinguish between possibility, probability, and truth. The language allows quantification over time points, probability values, and domain individuals. Probability is treated as a sentential operator in the language, so it can be arbitrarily nested and combined with other logical operators. Our model of possibility is similar to that presented by Pelavin [52]. Our model of chance in the context of branching time is based on that of van Fraassen [68]. The probabilistic component of our logic is similar to Halpern's [27] probability logic $\mathcal{L}_2$, to Bacchus's [5] logic of propositional probabilities, and to Haddawy and Frisch's [24] logic of staged probabilities.

1.1 Situation Calculus and State-Based Planning

The bulk of work on planning in AI has not taken the view outlined above. Most AI planning systems to date have used representations based on situation calculus [49]. This language is a variation of predicate calculus intended for representing time and change as a function of events by including explicit reference to situations in the language. A *situation* is a period of time over which no changes occur. Relations within a situation are states-of-affairs, which can be asserted to hold in a situation with a binary predicate T. For example, to say that block A is on block B in situation s_1 we write $T(ON(A, B), s_1)$. Situations are described by finite sets of sentences. For example, the situation in which block A is on block B which is on block C might be described by $T(ON(A, B), s_k) \wedge T(ON(B, C), s_k)$.

Transitions from one situation to another are made only through the execution of an action or occurrence of an event. So an action takes us from one situation to another. The effect of an action is represented by a function that maps an action and situation to the situation that results from performing the action. An example of an action might be the *UNSTACK* operator which removes one block from on top of another one and puts it on the table. The result of an action is described with the function Do. $Do(UNSTACK(x, y), s_3)$ denotes the situation that results from executing *UNSTACK(x,y)* in situation s_3. To say that if x is on y and x is clear then after the unstack operation, x is on the table and y is clear we might write:

$$T(ON(x, y), s) \wedge T(CLEAR(x), s) \rightarrow$$
$$T(ON - TABLE(x), Do(UNSTACK(x, y), s)) \wedge$$
$$T(CLEAR(y), Do(UNSTACK(x, y), s))$$

Situation calculus gave rise to the state-based planning paradigm, exemplified by such systems as STRIPS [18], NOAH [57], and HACKER [67]. In this paradigm, a planning problem is described in terms of an initial situation description, a goal formula, and a set of operators that describe actions by specifying transformations from one situation description to another. A plan is then any sequence of operators that transforms the initial situation description into a situation description that entails the goal. Systems like STRIPS are able to efficiently generate plans due to the severe constraints that the state-based representation places on the planning problem.

In the state-based paradigm, the environment is completely predictable since the state of the world is known with certainty, the agent's actions are deterministic, and all changes in the environment are due to the planning agent's actions. Since actions are instantaneous there is no concept of an action being influenced by conditions during its execution. Since only one action can occur between two situations, plans may not contain concurrent actions. Since goals only describe the final situation, there is no concept of goals with temporal extent. The state-based paradigm provides no meaningful notion of an approximate plan – a plan either achieves the goal or it doesn't. Approximation is an important concept in situations in which a system must respond in real time or within certain time constraints.

Finally, the state-based paradigm provides no notion of what constitutes rational behavior. This is a critical deficiency because the purpose of a planner is to recommend a course of action and we would like to know that this course of action is rational in some well-defined sense. So we seek a theory that provides a link between a system's representation of plans and the rationality of courses of action derived from that representation. Decision Theory will be shown to address exactly this problem, as well as the problem of representing uncertainty. But first we examine ways of representing temporal information in planning.

1.2 Temporal Logic

Researchers in AI have used temporal logics to represent various temporal aspects of planning problems not representable in the state-based planning paradigm. Temporal logics represent change by specifying what is true in the world at various times. Thus they can represent change brought about by events outside the agent's control. Temporal logics can be classified as being either interval or point-based. A point-based logic associates a time point with each temporal object. Most work on plan representation in AI has used interval-based logics which associate a time interval with each temporal object. Through the use of intervals, actions, events, and facts can have temporal extent. This means that these temporal languages can represent plans with concurrent actions as well as conditions during the execution of an action that influence the action. For this reason, the logic of time, chance, and action developed in this monograph uses time intervals as well.

Temporal logics can be further classified as being either linear or branching. Linear time logics [3, 1] model only the actual world and thus can only represent that an event actually occurs at a given time. In contrast, branching time logics [50, 22, 54] model all possible worlds and thus can represent whether or not an event can possibly occur, as well as its various possible times of occurrence. Since we are interested in representing chance, which can be roughly thought of as a degree of possibility, we will use a branching time logic. Chance is modeled by defining probability distributions over the branching time structure.

1.3 Decision Theory

Decision Theory addresses two of our primary concerns: the representation of uncertainty and the formalization of rational choice. Bayesian Decision Theory can be roughly defined as the study of the characterization and formalization of rational choice under uncertainty. The question of exactly what constitutes rational choice has been the subject of much debate. The most general definition of rationality is given by Maher [46]: "To say X is rational is to express one's acceptance of norms that permit X." So the central problem of Bayesian Decision Theory is to lay out a set of generally accepted norms governing an agent's choice behavior and to show that for a set of preferences consistent with those norms, there exist probability and utility functions such that in any given choice situation the alternative that maximizes expected utility is the preferred alternative. A theorem showing such a correspondence is called a *representation theorem*. Several examples of representation theorems can be found in the literature [56, 58, 35, 46]. Fishburn [19] presents a survey of representation theorems.

The use of Decision Theory as the semantic basis of a representation for planning gives us a mapping between the problem representation and the rationality of the behavior resulting from the use of the representation. More concretely, if a planner can be said to in some way be choosing plans that maximize expected utility then that planner's choices are rational with respect to some set of preferences. Note that the planner need not explicitly perform decision-theoretic analyses. It suffices that the planner act according the the recommendations that such analyses would make. We develop the link from the logic of time, chance, and action to the concept of rational choice by first developing the concept of expected utility for our logic and then by analyzing the relationship between planning to satisfy goals and planning to maximize expected utility.

A direct consequence of the use of expected utility to compare plans is that we have a useful notion of approximation. Each plan has an associated expected utility and an approximate plan is one which has a lower expected utility than the optimal plan. In time critical situations, inference time may be saved by choosing a plan that is not known to be optimal.

Unfortunately, Decision Theory does not provide all the representational capabilities needed for modeling planning problems.

- Decision-theoretic representations have traditionally been limited to propositional languages [55]. First-order quantification provides great representational economy by allowing us to describe properties shared by general classes of actions, events, and facts. For example, rather than having to define a different lifting action for each possible object, we can describe the class of lifting actions, where the object being lifted is left as a quantified variable.
- Decision theory provides no vocabulary for describing planning problems [71, p570]. We would like a language that facilitates representing the salient features of planning problems in such a way that desired inferences follow directly from the semantics of the language.
- Finally, Decision Theory has traditionally assumed that it is always within an agent's power to execute an action. This assumption is extremely limiting. First, it means that we must have a plan completely specified before it can be compared to other plans since we must know what it means to execute the plan in each possible state of the world. Second, it means that we cannot reason about plans based on descriptions of individual actions since plans

may contain actions that conflict and cannot be executed together.

This monograph addresses all of these limitations. We provide a language that allows quantification to be combined with statements about probability. The logic is structured in such a way that desired inferences follow directly from the semantics. The semantics imposes natural constraints on the assignment of probabilities to temporal actions, events, and facts. We extend the decision-theoretic framework to encompass actions that may not be feasible by first formalizing the concept of action feasibility and then defining a notion of expected utility for such actions.

1.4 Decision-Theoretic Planning

Work on applying decision-theoretic principles to planning problems can be roughly divided into development of plan generation algorithms, development of temporal projection algorithms, and formal work on representations. The work presented in this monograph falls into the last category.

Plan Generation Algorithms Work on decision-theoretic plan generation has employed either the STRIPS assumption or Markovian assumptions to reduce the complexity of the problem. The first three approaches discussed below make the STRIPS assumption, while the last two model the world as a Markov process. Wellman [76] has provided a formalization of the STRIPS assumption for probabilistic planning. He characterizes it as assuming that the agent's beliefs about changes in propositions not mentioned in an action's specification are independent of the action, given those effects explicitly specified. He formalizes this in terms of probabilistic independence.

The first AI researchers to cast the planning problem in a decision-theoretic framework were Feldman and Sproul [17]. They develop a framework for decision-theoretic planning in which they augment the basic STRIPS representation by introducing costs associated with actions, utilities of achieving goals, and probabilities over states. They present neither a planning algorithm nor an implementation.

The SUDO-PLANNER system [73, 74, 75] uses decision-theoretic principles to eliminate classes of suboptimal plans in domains characterized by partially satisfiable goals and actions with uncertain effects. It eliminates only those classes of plans which it can prove are dominated without resorting to reasoning about tradeoffs. Planning knowledge is represented in the form of qualitative probabilistic networks, which encode atemporal qualitative constraints on the joint probability distribution over a set of variables, as well as the qualitative relation of those variables to a value node. The planner's goal is to maximize the value node. Action effects are represented as qualitative relations among the action and event variables, with the temporal relations being implicit. Plans are functions from observations to actions. The planner works by cycling between the processes of model construction and dominance proving. Model construction involves constructing a qualitative probabilistic network from a more general knowledge base for the domain. Dominance proving involves using knowledge about the effects of actions and the relative desirability of outcomes to derive facts about the preferred plan.

Kushmerick, et.al. [41] present an algorithm for probabilistic planning. They extend the STRIPS action representation to allow conditional and probabilistic effects. The world is characterized as a probability distribution over possible states and actions cause a transition from one state distribution to another. The BURIDAN algorithm generates a plan that achieves a goal with a probability no less than a user-specified threshold. The algorithm, which is related to the SNLP algorithm [48] for planning in deterministic domains, alternates between the operations of plan assessment and plan refinement. Plan assessment involves determining whether the probability that the current plan achieves the goal exceeds the specified threshold. Plan refinement attempts to increase the probability of the goal by directly increasing the probability of a relevant condition or by decreasing the probability of a threat to a relevant condition. They prove the planner to be both sound and complete.

Drummond and Bresina [13] present an algorithm for generating plans in stochastic temporal domains. They represent the dynamics of the domain as a discrete Markov process, where actions and exogenous events are characterized by transition probabilities. Goals are temporally qualified sentences, so they can represent deadline, maintenance, and prevention goals. The algorithm works by first projecting a single path that satisfies the goal. In generating this path the system explores only likely outcomes, ignoring those of low probability. This produces a plan with a lower bound probability of achieving the goal. The probability of goal satisfaction can be increased by elaborating the plan with additional paths that satisfy the goal. So the algorithm can be consulted at any time after the initial plan is generated to obtain the best plan so far.

Dean, et.al. [8] present an algorithm, based on Markov decision theory, for planning with deadlines in stochastic domains. The world is modeled as a stochastic automaton consisting of a finite set of states; actions are represented by transition probabilities between states; goals are represented by reward functions over the states; and plans are policies that specify what action to perform in each state. The algorithm starts by generating a policy for a simplified world model. It then iteratively expands the world model and generates the optimal policy for each expanded model. The expected values of generated plans improve as a function of computation time and the algorithm can be consulted at any time after the initial policy is generated to obtain the best policy so far. They improve on the work of Drummond and Bresina by providing theoretically sound probabilistic foundations and by providing decision-theoretic methods for controlling inference.

Plan Projection Algorithms Temporal projection is the task of predicting the future state of the world given beliefs about the current state of the world and a set of events expected to occur. Although all the above plan generation algorithms do some kind of projection, research on projection algorithms attempts to develop more complex dynamic models without the restrictive assumptions made by the above systems.

Dean and Kanazawa [9] present an approach to projecting the effects of actions and events under uncertainty.[1] Time is represented as isomorphic to the integers. Knowledge of the world is represented in terms of probabilities that propositions are true at each time point. The tendency of propositions to remain true over time is modeled with conditional probability statements that indicate the probability that a proposition P is true at time t conditioned on whether or not P was true at the previous time point and whether or not an event know to make P true or false occurred in the interim. Uncertain relationships among the occurrence of events are expressed with conditional probability statements that specify the probability of an event occurring given the occurrence of a causing event and a set of causal preconditions. These two types of conditional probabilities are represented in the form of a probabilistic network which contains a node for each proposition and event of interest at every time point. Projection is performed using one of the standard inference algorithms for probabilistic networks.

Hanks [29, 30, 31] presents a system for projecting the effects of actions and events under uncertainty. Time is modeled as isomorphic to the integers. Knowledge of the world is represented in terms of probabilities that propositions are true at various time points, but not necessarily at every time point as in Dean and Kanazawa's approach. The dynamics of the world is modeled with causal rules that describe the tendency of a proposition to change state as a result of an event and with persistence rules that describe the chance that a proposition changes state over an interval during which no causally relevant event is known to occur. Actions can have uncertain conditional effects, including duration. The projector answers queries of the form "is the probability that ϕ will hold at time t greater than τ?" The algorithm is particularly distinguished by its efficiency, which it gains by searching only for past evidence relevant to the query and by making only relevant distinctions when projecting effects forward in time. In contrast, Dean and Kanazawa's approach computes the probability of every proposition at every point in time.

Plan Representations Work on the development of formal plan representations has focused on integrating the representation of uncertainty with that of time or action or both.

Kanazawa [37] presents a logic of time and probability. The language allows quantification over time points but is propositional otherwise. The focus of the logic is on representing the tendency of facts to persist through time. A fact is something that once it becomes true tends to stay true for some time. Facts are associated with temporal intervals. Events take place instantaneously and are associated with a single time point. The logic distinguishes three types of events. Persistence causation events are associated with a fact becoming true. Persistence termination events are associated with a fact becoming false. Point events

---

[1] The framework is also described by Dean and Wellman [12].

are facts that stay true for only an instant. Actions are represented as events. A model for the logic contains a collection of world-histories. The semantics of the probability operator is defined in terms of probability distributions over world-histories. The logic has a corresponding graphical representation called a time net, which is a kind of probabilistic network that encodes the probability of facts and events over time. The relation of Kanazawa's logic to the logic of time, chance, and action presented in this monograph is discussed fully in Section 10.2.

The closest work to that presented in this monograph is the propositional temporal probabilistic logic of Dean and Wellman [12]. They extend Shoham's propositional temporal logic [61] by introducing a probability operator. The temporal logic distinguishes liquid propositions which if true over an interval are true over any subinterval from event propositions which hold over the interval of the event's occurrence but over no proper subinterval. The language does not distinguish between actions and events. The probability operator can be combined freely with other logical operators. Like Kanazawa's logic, a model contains a set of possible time lines and the semantics of the probability operator is defined in terms of a probability measure over the time lines. The relation of Dean and Wellman's logic to the logic of time, chance, and action is discussed fully in Section 10.2.

Martin [47] presents a language for planning with statistics. He extends Allen's [2] event logic with the ability to express probability information in the form of α-level confidence intervals on events. He shows how to compute these confidence intervals from statistics on events. He provides a scheme for selecting the most specific action preconditions for which sufficient statistics are available to allow a decision to be made. He does not provide a precise model-theoretic semantics for the language nor a set of axioms.

Chrisman [7] introduces a method for probabilistic modeling of abstract actions. Since conditions influencing the outcomes of an action may include the planner's own previous actions and it is not reasonable to expect to have a distribution over the planner's own choices of action, he adopts an interval-based representation of uncertainty. He derives a closed-form projection rule that works by finding the convex hull of possible poststate probability distributions.

The logic of time, chance, and action presented in this monograph is distinguished from the above formal planning representations in several ways. It is the only of the logics that is fully first-order and the only one with a set of axioms. It is the only logic with a probability operator that is temporally indexed and which may be nested. It is the only of the above logics that represents both the concepts of probability and possibility. Finally, it is the only framework to formalize commonsense notions of time and chance and incorporate them into the semantics in such a way that desired inferences follow directly from model theory.

1.5 Desiderata

By integrating both time and chance into a common representational framework, we would expect to be able to represent the following aspects of planning problems:

1. uncertainty in the state of the world:
   There is a 60% chance of a power glitch between noon and 5:00.
2. uncertainty of action effects:
   There is a 50% chance that the coin will land heads if flipped.
3. conditions during an action that influence its effects:
   Holding the oven temperature constant while the souffle is being baked increases the likelihood that the souffle will turn out right.
4. conditions not influenced by an action:
   The chance of rain is independent of my clapping my hands.
5. concurrent actions:
   It is not possible for me to raise and lower my arm at the same time.
6. external events:
   There is a 90% chance that the computer will crash if a power glitch occurs.
7. temporally qualified goals:
   Be at the bank before 5:00pm.

Furthermore, the logic should provide the following capabilities.

8. The logic should provide a link between the representation of plans and the notion of rational choice.
9. The logic should capture the temporal properties of chance so that desired inferences follow directly from the semantics.
10. The language should allow us to describe the components of a planning problem in such a way that they can be composed to reason about plans. This allows us to break a complex problem into components, describe each component, and then compose them to obtain a solution to the original problem.

We will show that the logic of time, chance, and action developed in this monograph satisfies all of these desiderata.

1.6 Use of the Logic

The logic of time, chance, and action is intended to be used as a tool in the representation of a new class of interesting and difficult planning problems. It enables us to design planning algorithms for these problems and to prove the algorithms' correctness. This dissertation illustrates the use of the logic for the design and verification of planning systems by carrying through an instance of the methodology outlined below.

1. Design a specialized planning algorithm.
2. Represent the data structures as sentences in the logic.
3. Represent assumptions about the world implicit in the algorithm as axiom schemas in the logic.
4. Represent algorithmic steps as inferences over the sentences and axiom schemas.
5. Use the logic to prove the algorithm sound and possibly complete.

In addition to facilitating the verification of new planning systems, steps 2–5 can be used to analyze existing planners as well.

Proving the correctness of a given planning algorithm may be an extremely difficult task. But even if the above methodology is not followed through to its completion, representing the data structures and assumptions of a planner in our logic is a valuable exercise. It makes explicit and precise the meaning of the knowledge embodied in the planning algorithm in such a way that we can analyze what is entailed by this knowledge without reference to the planning algorithm itself.

1.7 Outline

The monograph is organized as follows. Chapter 2 presents the ontology of the logic. It discusses the desired properties of time, chance, and action at an intuitive level, without recourse to logical formalism. Chapter 3 formalizes the concepts discussed in the ontology by presenting the syntax and semantics of the logic. Constraints are imposed on the semantic model in order to obtain the desired intuitive properties. We show how the language achieves points 1–7 of the desiderata. Chapter 4 presents a proof theory for the logic and derives several useful theorems illustrating the use of the proof theory. Numerous axioms and theorems are statements of the intuitive properties discussed in the ontology, thus satisfying point 9 of the desiderata. Chapter 5 discusses how the logic can be used to describe properties of actions and plans. We show that the logic captures the natural temporal relation between cause and effect, another example of desiderata point 9. Chapter 6 develops the concept of expected utility for acts that may not be feasible and discusses the relationship between goals and utilities. The definition of expected utility provides the link between the logic and a theory of rational behavior, thus satisfying desiderata point 8. Chapter 7 shows how the logic can be used to describe and reason about planning problems. Planning problems are described by describing individual components of the problem. The separate descriptions are composed to reason about the overall problem. This demonstrates desiderata point 10. Chapter 8 demonstrates an instantiation of the above methodology by developing a specialized planning system for the problem of building construction planning and then analyzing it with the logic. Chapter 9 discusses related work, and Chap. 10 draws conclusions and points to directions for future research.

2 Ontology

In this chapter we seek to sharpen the reader's intuitions concerning those aspects of the world described by the logic of time, chance, and action. We specify the aspects of the world that the logic describes as well as their desired properties. The present work focuses on modeling five aspects of the world: time, facts/events, actions, possibility, and chance.

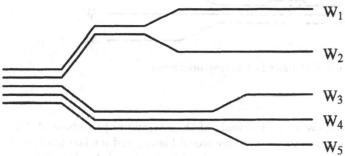

Fig. 1. The temporal tree.

2.1 Time

Time is modeled as a collection of world-histories, each of which is one possible chronology or history of events throughout time. At any given point in time, some of the world-histories will naturally share a common past up to that time. Thus the world-histories form a tree structure that branches into the future. No special status is given to the time "now", so the temporal tree branches into the future relative to each point in time. Figure 1 shows the structure of the temporal tree. The present work is only concerned with future-branching time because actions and events can only affect the state of the world at times after their occurrence. That is to say, at each point in time, the past is fixed—no occurrences in the world will cause it to change. But at each point in time the future might unfold in any number of ways, which are influenced by the agent's actions as well as by other events. So relative to any point in time, only one possible past exists, but numerous possible futures exist.[2]

2.2 Facts and Events

The world is described in terms of facts and events. Facts tend to hold and events tend to occur over intervals of time. So facts and events are associated with the time intervals over which they hold or occur in the various world-histories. Facts

---

[2] For a more thorough discussion of why a future-branching time model is appropriate for representing effects see the article by Mellor [51].

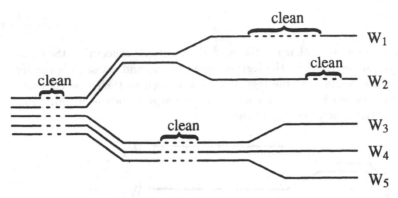

Fig. 2. Facts hold at different times in different branches.

are distinguished from events on the basis of their temporal properties. A fact may hold over several intervals in any given world-history and if a fact holds over an interval then it holds over all subintervals of that interval. So, for example, my car may be alternately clean and dirty over several different time periods in a given world-history and if my car is clean over a period of time, then it is clean throughout that time. Such a temporal tree is shown in Fig. 2.

Events are somewhat more complex than facts. First, one must distinguish between *event types* and *event tokens*. An event type is a general class of events and an event token is a specific instance of an event type. For example, picking up a book is an event type, and picking up the blue book on my desk at 9:00am is an event token of that type. So event types are sets of event tokens. Event tokens are unique individuals – the interval over which an event token occurs is the unique interval containing the event token and an event token can occur at most once in any world-history. If I pick up a book during a time period, there is no smaller period of time during which the event token of my picking up the book can be said to have occurred. On the other hand, numerous tokens of a given event type may occur during a particular interval. For example, I can pick up one book with my right hand and one with my left hand concurrently. So if a token of an event type occurs over an interval, it is possible for another token of that type to occur over a subinterval, but it is not necessary as it is in the case of facts. The present work deals with event types, which for brevity are simply referred to as events.

The fact/event dichotomy just described is a simplification of the true situation. As Shoham [61] has shown, there are many different types of facts and events, characterized by their temporal properties. Although Shoham's refined categories of fact types constitute a more useful and accurate picture of the world than the simple fact/event dichotomy, the fact/event categorization will be used for simplicity of exposition. Extending the work to encompass Shoham's categories is completely straightforward.

2.3 Actions

Actions are similar to events but are distinguished from events by the fact that
an action is brought about by an agent. We view the planning problem from
the perspective of the planning agent. From this perspective, only the planning
agent's own actions are acts. All other actions appear as events. An action is
initiated by an *attempt*: The agent attempts an action and, if conditions are
right, the action occurs. The occurrence of the action will have certain effects.
Likewise, if conditions are such that the attempt of the action does not result in
its occurrence, the attempt will have other effects.[3] The situation is depicted in
Fig. 3. Once an agent attempts an action, whether or not the action occurs is a
function of chance; furthermore, what effects the action's success or failure will
have is also a function of chance.

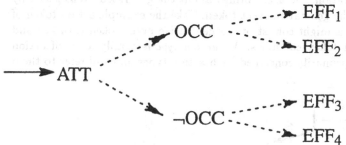

Fig. 3. Action representation.

Distinguishing the attempt of an action from its occurrence facilitates several
useful inferences. First, it facilitates reasoning about actions as goals. Examples
of such goals are going skiing or eating at one's favorite restaurant. In planning for such goals, we are interested in finding circumstances under which the
attempt of the action will result in its occurrence.

Second, separating the attempt of an action from its occurrence allows us to
distinguish between effects due to the occurrence from effects due to the attempt.
For example, lifting an object will result in the agent's holding it but attempting
to lift an object that is too heavy may result in the agent straining his back.
One advantage of being able to make this distinction is that we can distinguish
between a plan achieving a goal through its occurrence and a plan achieving a
goal as a side-effect of its attempt.

Third, the separation facilitates temporal reasoning about actions. Action
occurrences can span time, allowing us to reason about conditions during an
action. Furthermore, the amount of time required for an action to occur once it
is attempted can be allowed to vary, depending on conditions.

As with events, we distinguish action tokens and action types. Action tokens
and action types are analogous to event tokens and event types. Our representation of action tokens is based on Goldman's [21] theory of action. Goldman

---

[3] In AI the effects of the action's occurrence are typically called *intended effects* and
those of the action's failed attempt are typically called *side effects*.

presents a theory of action individuation in which he defines a generation relation that holds between certain actions. An act token A *generates* an act token A' if it can be said that A' was done by doing A. For example, "flipping the light switch" and "turning on the light" are related by generation. So rather than saying that the two are different descriptions of the same action or that they are two completely different actions, Goldman says that they are two different actions but are related by generation. Generally A and A' will be causally related but other relationships are also possible. Goldman [21, Ch 2] details four different relationships that he classifies as generation.

We define an *action token* to be composed of a *generative* event token, representing the action's attempt and a *generated* event token, representing the event associated with the successful occurrence of the action. The two event tokens are related by generation: the agent brings about the generated event token by bringing about by the generative event token. Take the example action token of starting my car. This might consist of the generative event token turn-key and the generated event token car-starts. An *action type* is simply a set of action tokens. We will be primarily concerned with action types and will refer to them simply as actions.

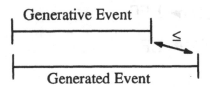

Fig. 4. Relative times of generative and generated events.

We impose constraints on the temporal relation between the generative events and the generated event of an action token. The beginning time of the generative event must coincide with the beginning time of the generated event and the end time of the generative event must not occur after the end time of the generated event. See Fig. 4.

2.4 Possibility

Because the present work is concerned with representing actions that affect the state of the world, the kind of possibility we are interested in describing is objective possibility. Something is objectively possible if it either was true in the past or could be true in the future. So possibility is taken relative to a point in time in the temporal tree. Since actions and events can only affect the future, conditions in the present and past relative to a given time are either inevitably true or inevitably false.

2.5 Chance

There is a subtle reason for distinguishing between possibility and chance. It is tempting to think that possibility could just be represented by saying that the probability is non-zero but this is not the case. The problem is that in an uncountably infinite sample space possible events can have probability zero. For example, suppose you pick a real number randomly in the interval [0 1]. For each number the probability that it will be picked is zero, yet it is possible that it will be picked. The ability to make this distinction will become essential when we discuss action feasibility in Chap. 5. Possibility and chance are related by the fact that impossibility implies probability zero and inevitability implies probability one.

Chance is introduced by defining probabilities over the tree of possible futures. Like possibility, chance is taken relative to a given point in time. As a consequence of the property that the past is inevitably true or inevitably false and the fact that inevitability implies probability one, it follows that the chance of the past is either zero or one. In this way, actions and other events can only affect the probabilities of future facts and events. This type of probability is objective, as opposed to subjective. Subjectively the past can be uncertain but objectively it is completely determined. For example, subjectively I may be uncertain as to whether the train has left or not, yet objectively it either certainly left or it certainly did not and, furthermore, there is nothing I can do now to change that. The other property imposed on objective chance is that the chance be completely determined by the history up to the current time. So objective chance is purely a function of the state of the world. In contrast, subjective probability is a function not only of the state of the world but also of the epistemic state of an agent.

The present characterization of objective chance is not to be confused with the frequentist interpretation of probability [69, 70] which is often called objective probability. Frequentist theories define probability in terms of the limiting relative frequency in an infinite number of trials or events. The current work does not rely on relative frequencies for its semantics. Rather it models objective chance by formalizing the properties that characterize objective chance. Thus while frequentist theories have difficulty assigning meaningful probabilities to unique events like a fish jumping out of the water at a given location and time, our model has no problem in assigning non-trivial probabilities to such events. Our model of chance is motivated by the subjectivist theories of objective chance [43, 64, 68], which define it in terms of properties that one would expect a rational agent to believe objective chance to possess. Although the current work does not include subjective probabilities, the model is completely consistent with the subjectivist framework.

This distinction between the frequentist theory of probability and our conception of objective chance puts the present work in sharp contrast with Bacchus's [4, 5] logic of statistical probabilities which models exactly relative frequency type probabilities. One telling difference between the two logics is that Bacchus's logic Lp assigns only probability 0 or 1 to unique events (more precisely, to all closed formulas). The present logic can assign any probability to unique events in the future, while events in the past are assigned only probability 0 or 1, as required by our definition of objective chance.

16

2.6 Planning

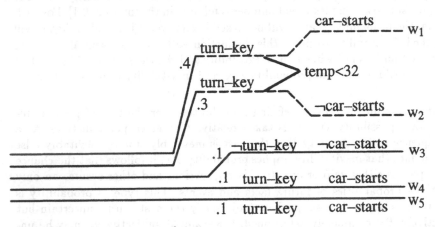

Fig. 5. Navigating the temporal tree.

Within the ontological framework just outlined planning becomes the task of navigating from the present to the future along a temporal tree in an effort to attain a world-history in which the goal condition is satisfied. If the assumptions inherent in the state-based planning paradigm are made in the current framework then an agent has complete control of its path along the tree: the state of the world is completely determined, actions have deterministic effects, and there are no external events to influence the agent's path. In the logic of time, chance, and action, on the other hand, an agent has only partial control over its path through the tree: there is uncertainty in the state of the world, action effects are not necessarily deterministic, and external events may influence the path of the agent.

For example, consider the temporal tree shown in Fig. 5. The temperature is below freezing in worlds w_1 and w_2 and above freezing in the rest of the worlds. So there is a 70% chance that the temperature is below freezing. The car is certain to start if the key is turned when the temperature is above freezing but there is only 57% chance that the car will start given that the key is turned when the temperature is below freezing. Thus, by turning the key, the agent can only partially control its path through the tree.

3 The Logic of Time, Chance, and Action

To formalize the concepts discussed in the ontology, we now define the language of the logic of time, chance, and action, $\mathcal{L}_{tca}$. First in order to provide a vocabulary for referring to the elements of our ontology, we specify the syntax of the language. The language of $\mathcal{L}_{tca}$ is a first-order language with modal operators to express possibility and chance. Since chance is treated as a sentential operator, it can be combined freely with other logical operators. The language allows quantification over probabilities, time points, and domain individuals. The syntax of the probabilistic component of the language is similar to that of Bacchus's [5] logic propositional probabilities and the syntax of the temporal component of the logic is based on both Shoham's [61] and Pelavin's [52] temporal logics.

The syntax provides only a formal way of writing down sentences in the language of $\mathcal{L}_{tca}$. We need some way of assigning meaning to these sentences. This is done through the use of model-theoretic semantics. The elements of our models correspond closely to the elements identified in the ontology. The models contain a set of possible world-histories as well as sets of facts, events, and actions. The temporal tree structure is created by defining an accessibility relation over the world-histories. Possibility is then defined with respect to this accessibility relation. Chance is defined in terms of probability distributions over the temporal tree. The desired properties identified in the ontology are obtained by placing a number of semantic constraints on the models.

3.1 Syntax

The language of $\mathcal{L}_{tca}$ contains four predicates. To refer to facts and event types occurring in time, the language contains two predicates: $HOLDS(FA, t_1, t_2)$ is true if fact FA holds over the time interval t_1 to t_2, and $OCCURS(EV, t_1, t_2)$ is true if event EV occurs during the interval t_1 to t_2. Henceforth we will use the symbol t, possibly subscripted, to denote time points; ϕ, ψ, and γ to denote formulas; and α and β to denote probability values.

The language contains two predicates to describe actions: $ATT(A, t_A)$ is true if action A is attempted beginning at time t_A, and $OCC(A, t_A, t'_A)$ is true if action A occurs during the interval t_A to t'_A.

In addition to the usual first-order logical operators, the language contains three modal operators to express inevitability, possibility, and chance. The operators are subscripted with a time since according to the ontology possibility, inevitability, and chance are taken relative to a point in time. We write $\Box_t(\phi)$ to indicate that ϕ is inevitably true at time t and $\Diamond_t(\phi)$ to say that ϕ is possibly true at time t. We write $P_t(\phi)$ to denote the probability of ϕ at time t. Probability is treated as a sentential operator in the object language. So the probability operator can be arbitrarily nested and combined with the inevitability operator, allowing us to write complex sentences like:

$$P_{t_1}(\Box_{t_2}\phi \wedge P_{t_3}(\psi) = \alpha) = \beta.$$

Such a treatment is useful for writing sentences about conditional probability. The probability of ϕ given ψ is traditionally defined as

$$prob(\phi|\psi) = prob(\phi \wedge \psi)/prob(\psi).$$

If the probability of the conditioning sentence ψ is zero, then the conditional probability is undefined. In this case, a conditional probability sentence like $prob(\phi|\psi) = \alpha$ can be assigned neither the value true nor the value false. Rather than introducing a new conditional probability operator and dealing with this truth assignment problem, sentences about conditional probability can simply be written in the form

$$P_t(\phi \wedge \psi)=\alpha \cdot P_t(\psi).$$

Note that this sentence is true for all values of α if $P_t(\psi) = 0$. The standard conditional probability notation will be used to syntactically denote a sentence of the above form:

Definition 1. c-prob

$$P_t(\phi|\psi)=\alpha \equiv P_t(\phi \wedge \psi)=\alpha \cdot P_t(\psi)$$

The language of $\mathcal{L}_{tca}$ contains three types of terms: ordinary domain object terms, temporal terms, and probability terms and four types of relations: numeric relations, fact relations, event relations, and action relations.

The *lexicon* of the language consists of the following disjoint sets of nonlogical symbols:

C a set of object constant symbols;
TC, a set of time constant symbols;
NC, a set of numeric constant symbols;
V, a set of object variables;
TV, a set of temporal variables;
PV, a set of probability variables;
FCT, a set of object function symbols;
$NFCT$, a set of numeric function symbols, including $+, -, \cdot, /$;
$PFCT$, a set of probability function symbols for representing distribution functions;
FR, a set of fact relation symbols;
ER, a set of event relation symbols;
AR, a set of action relation symbols; and
NR, the set $\{<, \leq, =, \geq, >\}$ of numeric relation symbols.

Note that we will use the symbols $<, \leq, =, \geq, >$ to denote numeric relations in both the object and the meta language. It will be clear from context which interpretation is meant.

The set of well-formed formulas combining the logical and nonlogical symbols is recursively defined as follows.

1. The set of *object terms* (o-terms) contains members of C, all members of V, as well as all terms of the form $f(otrm_1, ..., otrm_n)$, where $f \in FCT$ and $otrm_1, ..., otrm_n$ are o-terms.

2. The set of *temporal terms* (t-terms) contains all members of TC, all members of TV, as well as all terms of the form $f(ttrm_1, ..., ttrm_n)$, where $f \in NFCT$ and $ttrm_1, ..., ttrm_n$ are t-terms.

3. The set of *probability terms* (p-terms) contains all members of NC, all members of PV, all terms of the form $f(trm_1, ..., trm_n)$, where $f \in PFCT \cup NFCT$ and $trm_1, ..., trm_n$ are t-terms or p-terms, as well as all terms of the form $P_{ttrm}(\phi)$, where ϕ is a wff and $ttrm$ is a t-term.

4. If trm_1, trm_2 are both t-terms or p-terms then $ttrm_1 < ttrm_2$ is a wff, and similarly for $\leq, =, \geq, >$.

5. If $ttrm_1, ttrm_2$ are t-terms, $trm_1, ..., trm_n$ are o-terms or t-terms, and fr is an n-ary fact relation symbol then $HOLDS(fr(trm_1, ..., trm_n), ttrm_1, ttrm_2)$ is a wff.

6. If $ttrm_1, ttrm_2$ are t-terms, $trm_1, ..., trm_n$ are o-terms or t-terms, and er is an n-ary event relation symbol then $OCCURS(er(trm_1, ..., trm_n), ttrm_1, ttrm_2)$ is a wff.

7. If $ttrm_1$ is a t-term, $trm_1, ..., trm_n$ are o-terms or t-terms, and ar is an n-ary action relation symbol then $ATT(ar(trm_1, ..., trm_n), ttrm_1)$ is a wff.

8. If $ttrm_1, ttrm_2$ are t-terms, $trm_1, ..., trm_n$ are o-terms or t-terms, and ar is an n-ary action relation symbol then $OCC(ar(trm_1, ..., trm_n), ttrm_1, ttrm_2)$ is a wff.

9. If $otrm_1, otrm_2$ are o-terms then $otrm_1 = otrm_2$ is a wff.

10. If ϕ_1 and ϕ_2 are wff's then so are $\neg\phi_1$, $\phi_1 \wedge \phi_2$, $\phi_1 \vee \phi_2$, and $\phi_1 \rightarrow \phi_2$.

11. If ϕ is a wff and $z \in V \cup TV \cup PV$ then $\forall z \phi$ and $\exists z \phi$ are wff's.

12. If ϕ is a wff and $ttrm$ is a t-term then $\Box_{ttrm}(\phi)$ and $\Diamond_{ttrm}(\phi)$ are wffs.

We use the symbol $=$ to denote equality between object terms, probability terms, and temporal terms. The meaning will be clear from the context.

Notice that the syntax of the language is restricted to disallow sentences that would be meaningless in the intended interpretation of the language. For example the following sentence is not well-formed because it does not make sense for a probability term to be used as a time point:

$$HOLDS(ON(A,B), t_1, P_{t_1}(\phi)).$$

Desiderata Revisited. Now that we have defined the syntax of the language, we can revisit the desiderata outlined in the introduction and see how the language can represent the different types of planning knowledge. The language allows us to write sentences that describe

1. uncertainty in the state of the world:
   There is a 60% chance of a power glitch between noon and 5:00.
   $P_{now}(\exists t_1, t_2(noon \leq t_1 \leq t_2 \leq 5{:}00) \wedge OCCURS(\text{power-glitch}, t_1, t_2)) = .6$

2. uncertainty of action effects:

There is a 50% chance that the coin will land heads when flipped.
$$\forall t, t_1, t_2 \, (t \leq t_1) \; \rightarrow \; P_t(\exists t_3 \, OCCURS(\text{land}(\text{coin,heads}), t_2, t_3) \,| $$
$$OCC(\text{flip}(\text{coin}), t_1, t_2)) = .5$$

3. conditions during an action that influence its effects:

Holding the oven temperature constant increases the likelihood that the souffle will turn out right.
$$\forall t, t_1, t_2 \, (t \leq t_1) \; \rightarrow$$
$$P_t(\exists t_3 \, HOLDS(\text{done-right}(\text{souffle}), t_2, t_3) \,|$$
$$OCCURS(\text{bake}(\text{souffle}), t_1, t_2) \wedge \exists x \, HOLDS(\text{temp}(\text{oven},x), t_1, t_2)) >$$
$$P_t(\exists t_3 \, HOLDS(\text{done-right}(\text{souffle}), t_2, t_3) \,| OCCURS(\text{bake}(\text{souffle}), t_1, t_2))$$

4. conditions not influenced by an action:

The chance of rain is independent of my clapping my hands.
$$\forall t, t_1, t_2, t_3, t_4 \, (t_1 \leq t_3) \; \rightarrow$$
$$P_t(HOLDS(\text{raining}, t_3, t_4) | OCC(\text{clap}, t_1, t_2)) \; = \; P_t(HOLDS(\text{raining}, t_3, t_4))$$

5. concurrent actions:

It is not possible for me to raise and lower my arm at the same time.
$$\forall t, t_1, t_2, t_3, t_4$$
$$\Box_t[OCC(\text{raise}(\text{arm}), t_1, t_2) \wedge OCC(\text{lower}(\text{arm}), t_3, t_4) \rightarrow (t_2 < t_3) \vee (t_4 < t_1)]$$

6. external events:

There is a 90% chance that the computer will crash if a power glitch occurs.
$$\forall t_1, t_2 \, P_{now}(\exists t_3, t_4 \, (t_1 < t_3 \leq t_2) \wedge OCCURS(\text{crash}(\text{computer}), t_3, t_4) \,|$$
$$OCCURS(\text{power-glitch}, t_1, t_2)) = .9$$

7. temporally qualified goals:

Be at the bank before 5:00pm.
$$\exists t_1, t_2 \, (t_1 < 5:00) \wedge HOLDS(\text{loc}(\text{me,bank}), t_1, t_2)$$

Furthermore, the language allows us to write sentences that

- combine possibility and chance:

  There is a 50% chance that by noon a train crash will inevitably occur between 3:00 and 5:00.
  $$P_{now}(\exists t_1 \, (t_1 \leq noon) \wedge$$
  $$\Box_{t_1}(\exists t_2, t_3 (3:00 \leq t_2 \leq t_3 \leq 5:00) \wedge OCCURS(\text{crash}(\text{train}), t_2, t_3))) = .5$$

- distinguish between truth and chance:

  I won the lottery even though it was unlikely.
  $$(t_0 < t_1 < t_2 < now) \wedge$$
  $$P_{t_0}(OCCURS(\text{win-lottery}, t_1, t_2)) = .0001 \wedge OCCURS(\text{win-lottery}, t_1, t_2)$$

- express information about probability distributions:

  The arrival time of the train is normally distributed about noon.
  $$\forall t \, P_{now}(\exists t' \, OCCURS(\text{arrive}, t, t')) = N(t, noon, 10\text{min}),$$
  where $N(t, noon, 10\text{min})$ is a normal distribution over the variable t with mean noon and variance 10min.

3.2 Semantics

So far we have only specified a formal way of writing down sentences in the language of $\mathcal{L}_{tca}$. We need some way of assigning meaning to these sentences. This is done through the use of model-theoretic semantics. Note that the elements of the model correspond closely to the elements identified in the ontology.

A model is a tuple $\langle W, D, FN, NFN, PFN, FRL, ERL, ARL, NRL, FA, EVENTS, EV, ACTS, ACTIONS, R, \mathcal{X}, PR, F \rangle$, where:

- W is the set of possible world-histories, called worlds.
- D is the non-empty domain of individuals.
- FN is the set of object functions: $D^k \rightarrow D$.
- NFN is the set of numeric functions: $\Re^k \rightarrow \Re$.
- PFN is the set of probability functions: $\Re^k \rightarrow \Re$.
- FRL is the set of fact relations: $D^k \rightarrow 2^{(\Re \times \Re) \times W}$.
- ERL is the set of event relations: $D^k \rightarrow 2^{(\Re \times \Re) \times W}$.
- ARL is the set of action relations: $D^k \rightarrow 2^{ACTS}$.
- NRL is the set of numeric relations, a subset of $2^{\Re^k}$.
- FA is the set of facts, a subset of $2^{(\Re \times \Re) \times W}$. A fact is a set of $\langle$temporal interval, world$\rangle$ pairs: $\{\langle\langle t_1, t'_1\rangle, w_1\rangle, ..., \langle\langle t_n, t'_n\rangle, w_n\rangle\}$. If fa is a fact and $\langle\langle t_1, t_2\rangle, w\rangle \in fa$ then fa holds throughout interval $\langle t_1, t_2\rangle$ in world-history w.
- $EVENTS$ is the set of event tokens, a subset of $(\Re \times \Re) \times W$. An event token is a single $\langle$temporal interval, world$\rangle$ pair.
- EV is the set of event types, a subset of 2^{EVENTS}. An event type is a set of event tokens: $\{\langle\langle t_1, t'_1\rangle, w_1\rangle, ..., \langle\langle t_n, t'_n\rangle, w_n\rangle\}$. If ev is an event and $\langle\langle t_1, t_2\rangle, w\rangle \in ev$ then ev occurs during interval $\langle t_1, t_2\rangle$ in world-history w.
- $ACTS$ is the set of action tokens, a subset of $2^{EV \times EV}$. An action token is an ordered pair consisting of a generative event token and a generated event token: $\langle gev, Gev \rangle$. We will find it useful to define two functions in the meta-language in order to pick-out the generative and generated event tokens: $gen(act)$ is the generative event token of act and $Gen(act)$ is the generated event token of act.
- $ACTIONS$ is the set of action types, a subset of 2^{ACTS}. An action type is a set of action tokens: $\{\langle gev_1, Gev_1 \rangle, \langle gev_2, Gev_2 \rangle, ...\}$. For example, the start-car action might be represented as $\{\langle\langle \text{turn-key}, t_1, t_2\rangle, \langle \text{car-starts}, t_1, t_3\rangle\rangle, ...\}$. Note that the action type, event type, and fact corresponding to the empty set denote the impossible action, event, and fact, respectively.
- R is an accessibility relation defined on $\Re \times W \times W$. $R(t, w_1, w_2)$ means that world-histories w_1 and w_2 are indistinguishable up to and including time t. Making worlds indistinguishable through time t disallows instantaneous effects, i.e. there must be some time between the occurrence of an event and its effects. If $R(t, w_1, w_2)$ we say a world-history w_2 is R-accessible from w_1 at time t. The set of all world-histories R-accessible from w at time t will be designated R_t^w. For each time t, the R_t^w partition the world-histories into sets of equivalence classes indistinguishable up to t.

- $\mathcal{X}$ is a σ-algebra over W^4, containing all the sets corresponding to wff's in the language, as well as all R-equivalence classes of world-histories.
- PR is a probability assignment function that assigns to each time $t \in \Re$ and world-history $w \in W$ a countably additive probability distribution μ_t^w defined over $\mathcal{X}$.
- F is the denotation function, defined as follows:

  $C \rightarrow D,$
  $NC \rightarrow \Re,$
  $TC \rightarrow \Re,$
  $FCT \rightarrow FN,$
  $NFCT \rightarrow NFN,$
  $PFCT \rightarrow PFN,$
  $FR \rightarrow FRL,$
  $ER \rightarrow ERL,$
  $NR \rightarrow NRL.$

Henceforth, M will be used to refer a model with the eighteen components named above.

The reader will note that constants, functions, and relations are rigid with respect to both time and world-history. Rigidity with respect to world-history simplifies the logic somewhat and could be relaxed without much effort. Non-rigidity with respect to time seems to be basically incompatible with the current framework since it would result in inconsistencies like the following. At time t_1 a term like *Blue(car)* could denote the fact that my car is blue from t_0 to t_3 and at time t_2 it could denote the fact that my car is blue from t_4 to t_5.

Semantic Constraints. In Chap. 2 the ontology of the logic was discussed from an intuitive standpoint. In order to obtain the desired intuitive properties, a number of constraints must be imposed on the models. These constraints, labeled (C1)–(C8) are presented in the following discussion.

The future branching temporal tree is defined in terms of the R relation over world-histories. To capture the property that time does not branch into the past, we say that if two world-histories are indistinguishable up to time t_2 then they are indistinguishable up to any earlier time:

(C1) If $t_1 \leq t_2$ and $R(t_2, w_1, w_2)$ then $R(t_1, w_1, w_2)$.

Since R just represents the indistinguishability of histories up to a time t, for a fixed time R is an equivalence relation, i.e., reflexive, symmetric, and transitive:

(C2) $R(t, w, w)$
  If $R(t, w_1, w_2)$ then $R(t, w_2, w_1)$
  If $R(t, w_1, w_2)$ and $R(t, w_2, w_3)$ then $R(t, w_1, w_3)$

---

[4] A σ-algebra over W is a class of subsets that contains W and is closed under complement and countable union.

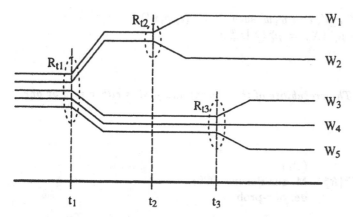

Fig. 6. Structure imposed by the R accessibility relation.

Figure 6 illustrates that the R relation ties together the different world-histories to form the temporal tree structure discussed in Chap. 2.

As mentioned earlier, facts and events differ in their temporal properties. This distinction is captured by the following two semantic constraints. If a fact holds over an interval, it holds over all subintervals, except possibly at the endpoints:

(C3) If $t_1 \leq t_2 \leq t_3 \leq t_4$, $t_1 \neq t_3$, $t_2 \neq t_4$, $fa \in FA$
and $\langle \langle t_1, t_4 \rangle, w \rangle \in fa$ then $\langle \langle t_2, t_3 \rangle, w \rangle \in fa$.

An event token occurs only once in each world-history:

(C4) If $evt \in EVENTS$, $\langle \langle t_1, t_2 \rangle, w \rangle \in evt$, and $\langle \langle t_3, t_4 \rangle, w \rangle \in evt$ then $t_1 = t_3$
and $t_2 = t_4$.

If two worlds are indistinguishable up to a time then they must share a common past up to that time. And if they share a common past up to a given time, they must agree on all facts and events up to that time. To enforce this relationship, we impose the constraint that if two world-histories are R-accessible at time t, they must agree on all facts(events) that hold(occur) over intervals ending before or at the same time as t:

(C5) If $t_0 \leq t_1 \leq t_2$ and $R(t_2, w_1, w_2)$ then $\langle \langle t_0, t_1 \rangle, w_1 \rangle \in A$ iff $\langle \langle t_0, t_1 \rangle, w_2 \rangle \in A$,
where A is a fact or event.

Chapter 2 mentions two desired characteristics of the probability operator. The first is that the probability at a time t be completely determined by the history up to that time. The second desired characteristic is that the probability of the present and past should be either zero or one, depending on whether or not it actually happened. These two properties follow as meta-theorems from the following two constraints:

(C6) For all $X \in \mathcal{X}, t \leq t'$, and w, w' such that $R(t, w, w')$,
$$\mu_t^w(R_{t'}^{w'}) > 0 \rightarrow \mu_{t'}^{w'}(X) = \mu_t^w(X | R_{t'}^{w'}).$$

(C7) $\mu_t^w(R_t^w) > 0.$

Meta-theorem 2 *The probability of the present and past is either zero or one.*

$$\mu_t^w(R_t^w) = 1$$

1. $\mu_t^w(R_t^w) > 0$ (C7)
2. $\mu_t^w(R_t^w) = \mu_t^w(R_t^w | R_t^w)$ Modus Ponens: (C6),1
3. $\mu_t^w(R_t^w) = 1$ def of c-prob

Defining the probabilities in this way makes good intuitive sense if we look at the meaning of R. R_t^w designates the set of world-histories that are objectively possible with respect to w at time t. It is natural that the set of world-histories that are objectively likely with respect to w at time t should be a subset of the ones that are possible.

Meta-theorem 3 *If two worlds are indistinguishable up to time t then they have identical probability distributions at that time.*

$$\text{If } R(t, w, w') \text{ then } \mu_t^{w'}(X) = \mu_t^w(X)$$

1. $\mu_t^w(R_t^{w'}) > 0$ (C2), (C7)
2. $\mu_t^w(R_t^{w'}) = \mu_t^w(X | R_t^{w'})$ Modus Ponens: (C6),1
3. $\mu_t^w(X | R_t^{w'}) = \mu_t^w(X | R_t^w)$ (C2)
4. $\mu_t^w(R_t^w) = 1$ Meta-theorem 2
5. $\mu_t^{w'}(X) = \mu_t^w(X)$ def of c-prob

The following constraint on actions performs two functions. First, it enforces the desired temporal relation between generative and generated event tokens. Second it guarantees that actions can actually occur, by requiring that the generative and generated event tokens of an action token occur in the same world-history.

(C8) If $act \in ACTS$ and $\langle \langle t_1, t_2 \rangle, w_1 \rangle = gen(act)$ and $\langle \langle t_3, t_4 \rangle, w_2 \rangle = Gen(act)$ then $t_1 = t_3, t_2 \leq t_4$, and $w_1 = w_2$.

Semantic Definitions. Given the models described above, the semantic definitions for the well-formed formulas can now be defined. Denotations are assigned to expressions relative to a model, a world-history within the model, and an assignment of individuals in the domain to variables. The denotation of an expression ϕ relative to a model M and a world-history w, and a variable assignment g is designated by $[\![\phi]\!]^{M,w,g}$. The variable assignment function g maps each temporal and probability variable to a real number and each object variable to a domain individual. In the definitions below, the expression $g[d/z]$ denotes the assignment of values to variables that is identical to assignment g with the possible exception that element d is assigned to variable z. The semantic definitions for the well-formed formulas are given below. The definitions specify the conditions under which sentences are assigned the value true. Since we have a two-valued logic, if a sentence is not true it is false.

1. If u is a variable then $[\![u]\!]^{M,w,g} = g(u)$.
2. If α is a non-logical constant then $[\![\alpha]\!]^{M,w,g} = F(\alpha)$.
3. If $\tau = f(trm_1, ..., trm_n)$ is a o-term, t-term, or p-term then
$$[\![\tau]\!]^{M,w,g} = [\![f]\!]^{M,w,g}([\![trm_1]\!]^{M,w,g}, ..., [\![trm_n]\!]^{M,w,g}).$$
4. $[\![trm_1 < trm_2]\!]^{M,w,g} = $ true iff $[\![trm_1]\!]^{M,w,g} < [\![trm_2]\!]^{M,w,g}$.
5. $[\![trm_1 = trm_2]\!]^{M,w,g} = $ true iff $[\![trm_1]\!]^{M,w,g} = [\![trm_2]\!]^{M,w,g}$.
6. $[\![HOLDS(rf(trm_1, ..., trm_n), ttrm_1, ttrm_2)]\!]^{M,w,g} = $ true iff
$\langle\langle[\![ttrm_1]\!]^{M,w,g}, [\![ttrm_2]\!]^{M,w,g}\rangle, w\rangle \in F(rf)([\![trm_1]\!]^{M,w,g}, ..., [\![trm_n]\!]^{M,w,g})$.
7. $[\![OCCURS(re(trm_1, ..., trm_n), ttrm_1, ttrm_2)]\!]^{M,w,g} = $ true iff
$\langle\langle[\![ttrm_1]\!]^{M,w,g}, [\![ttrm_2]\!]^{M,w,g}\rangle, w\rangle \in e$ for some
$e \in F(re)([\![trm_1]\!]^{M,w,g}, ..., [\![trm_n]\!]^{M,w,g})$.
8. $[\![ATT(ra(trm_1, ..., trm_n), ttrm_1)]\!]^{M,w,g} = $ true iff
$\exists act \in F(ra)([\![trm_1]\!]^{M,w,g}, ..., [\![trm_n]\!]^{M,w,g})$ such that
$\exists t\ gen(act) = \langle\langle[\![ttrm1]\!]^{M,w,g}, t\rangle, w\rangle$.
9. $[\![OCC(ra(trm_1, ..., trm_n), ttrm_1, ttrm_2)]\!]^{M,w,g} = $ true iff
$\exists act \in F(ra)([\![trm_1]\!]^{M,w,g}, ..., [\![trm_n]\!]^{M,w,g})$ such that
$\exists t\ gen(act) = \langle\langle[\![ttrm1]\!]^{M,w,g}, t\rangle, w\rangle$ and
$Gen(act) = \langle\langle[\![ttrm_1]\!]^{M,w,g}, [\![ttrm_2]\!]^{M,w,g}\rangle, w\rangle$.
10. $[\![\neg\phi]\!]^{M,w,g} = $ true iff $[\![\phi]\!]^{M,w,g} \neq $ true.
11. $[\![\phi_1 \wedge \phi_2]\!]^{M,w,g} = $ true iff $[\![\phi_1]\!]^{M,w,g} = $ true and $[\![\phi_2]\!]^{M,w,g} = $ true.
12. $[\![\forall z\ \phi]\!]^{M,w,g} = $ true iff $z \in V$ and $[\![\phi]\!]^{M,w,g[d/z]} = $ true for all $d \in D$ or $z \in TV \cup PV$ and $[\![\phi]\!]^{M,w,g[d/z]} = $ true for all $d \in \Re$.
13. $[\![\Box_{ttrm}(\phi)]\!]^{M,w,g} = $ true iff $[\![\phi]\!]^{M,w',g} = $ true for every w' such that $R([\![ttrm]\!]^{M,w,g}, w, w')$.
14. $[\![P_{ttrm}(\phi)]\!]^{M,w,g} = \mu^w_{[\![ttrm]\!]^{M,w,g}}(\{w' \in R^w_{[\![ttrm]\!]^{M,w,g}} : [\![\phi]\!]^{M,w',g} = $ true$\})$.

The logical operators $\vee$, $\rightarrow$, and $\exists$ are defined in terms of $\neg$, $\wedge$, and $\forall$ in the usual way. The numeric relations $\leq, =, \geq, >$ are defined in terms of $<$, e.g.,

$$(A \leq B) \equiv \neg(B < A).$$

Possibility $\Diamond$ is defined in terms of inevitability as $\Diamond_t(\phi) \equiv \neg\Box_t(\neg\phi)$. The interesting definitions are the last two. Definition 13 says that a sentence is inevitable in a world w at a time t iff it is true in all worlds indistinguishable from w up to time t. Definition 14 says that the probability of a sentence ϕ in a world w at a time t is the probability of those accessible worlds in which ϕ is true.

A sentence ϕ is *satisfied* by a model M at a world w if it is assigned the value true by that model and world. A sentence is *valid* if it is satisfied by every model at every world. The value assignment g is irrelevant the the truth value of a sentence since by definition sentences contain no free variables.

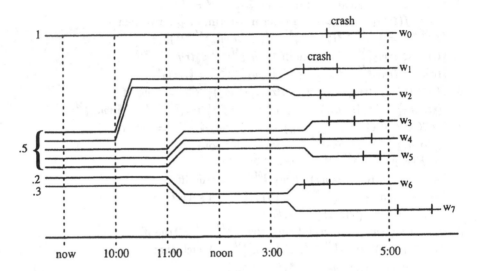

Fig. 7. Model for train crash example.

3.3 Example

To illustrate the correspondence between the syntax and semantics of $\mathcal{L}_{tca}$ we show a possible model for one of the example sentences presented earlier:

- There is a 50% chance that by noon a train crash will inevitably occur between 3:00 and 5:00.

$$P_{now}(\exists t_1\,(t_1 \leq noon)\, \wedge$$
$$\Box_{t_1}(\exists t_2, t_3(3{:}00 \leq t_2 \leq t_3 \leq 5{:}00) \wedge OCCURS(\text{crash}(\text{train}), t_2, t_3))) = .5$$

One possible model for this sentence is shown in Fig. 7. The sentence is not satisfied in world w_0 since there the chance that a crash between 3:00 and 5:00 is inevitable by noon is one. The sentence is satisfied in worlds w_1–w_7. In worlds w_1 and w_2 a crash between 3:00 and 5:00 is inevitable at 10:00am. In each of the worlds $w_3 - w_5$ a crash between 3:00 and 5:00 is inevitable at 11:00am. The chance of worlds $w_1 - w_5$ is 50%. In worlds w_6 and w_7 a crash is inevitable but it does not necessarily occur between 3:00 and 5:00. In worlds w_1–w_7 there is a 70% chance of a crash occurring between 3:00 and 5:00. This is higher than the chance of the crash inevitably occurring. Notice that it follows from the above sentence that there is a 50% chance an agent controlling the train can do nothing to avoid a crash after noon.

4 Proof Theory

In this chapter we present a partial axiomatization for $\mathcal{L}_{tca}$. We then use the axiomatization to prove numerous theorems that illustrate properties of the logic and that will be useful later in reasoning about actions and plans. In addition to facilitating reasoning with the logic, the axioms and theorems presented in this chapter show that the constraints imposed on the models in Chap. 3 are sufficient to capture the desired intuitive properties described in the ontology.

Before presenting the axioms we first note that $\mathcal{L}_{tca}$ is not completely axiomatizable. This fact follows from a result due to Halpern [27]. Halpern presents a first-order probability logic $\mathcal{L}_2$ that allows quantification over real probability values and domain individuals. The language of $\mathcal{L}_2$ is that of ordinary first-order logic with the addition of the probability operator P. Probability in models for $\mathcal{L}_2$ is defined in terms of a single distribution over possible worlds. Halpern shows that the valid formulas of $\mathcal{L}_2$ are not recursively enumerable and hence the logic is not completely axiomatizable. The argument that this entails the non-axiomatizability of $\mathcal{L}_{tca}$ is given below.

Sentences of $\mathcal{L}_2$ can be translated to sentences of $\mathcal{L}_{tca}$ as follows. Halpern's P operator is translated as a probability at a given fixed time, say t_0: P_{t_0}. All atomic formulas are translated as instantaneous facts at that same fixed time, e.g., on(A,B) becomes $HOLDS(\text{on(A,B)}, t_0, t_0)$. So, for example, the $\mathcal{L}_2$ sentence

$$\forall x\, P(\exists y\, Q(x,y) \wedge P(\forall z\, R(z)) = .7) = .2$$

would be translated as

$$\forall x\, P_{t_0}(\exists y\, HOLDS(Q(x,y), t_0, t_0) \wedge P_{t_0}(\forall z\, HOLDS(R(z), t_0, t_0)) = .7) = .2$$

Now an $\mathcal{L}_{tca}$ sentence which is a translation of an $\mathcal{L}_2$ sentence is valid in our logic if and only if the corresponding $\mathcal{L}_2$ sentence is valid in Halpern's logic. So if the valid formulas of $\mathcal{L}_{tca}$ were recursively enumerable so would be the valid formulas of $\mathcal{L}_2$. Since the valid formulas of $\mathcal{L}_2$ are not recursively enumerable, the valid formulas of $\mathcal{L}_{tca}$ cannot be either. Hence $\mathcal{L}_{tca}$ is not completely axiomatizable.

The lack of existence of a complete axiomatization for $\mathcal{L}_{tca}$ is not seen as a serious drawback for two reasons. First, the logic is intended to be used in the design and analysis of planning algorithms that are sound with respect to the logic and possibly complete with respect to a subset of the logic. In fact, the author knows of no planning algorithms that are complete even for first-order logic. Second, a sound set of axioms and rules of inference can be provided that are rich enough to allow us to make all inferences considered in this monograph.

4.1 Axioms

The axioms presented below are divided into classes. First there are six basic classes describing six types of reasoning:

1. first-order axioms with equality and the rules of Modus Ponens and Universal Generalization to describe first-order logical reasoning,

2. axioms of real closed fields to describe numeric reasoning,
3. S5 axioms and the rule of necessitation for reasoning about inevitability,
4. probability axioms and the rule of probability of logical equivalents to describe probabilistic reasoning,
5. temporal logic axioms to describe temporal reasoning, and
6. an action axiom for reasoning about action.

Following these are three sets of axioms that relate some of the basic classes:

– the inevitability and equality axiom,
– axioms describing the temporal properties of inevitability, and
– axioms relating inevitability and probability.

Subsets of the axioms have appeared elsewhere in the literature as parts of axiomatizations of other logics. The first-order axioms and rules of inference are taken from [34][Chap. 1] and appear originally in [78]. The S5 axioms and rule of necessitation are taken from [34][Chap. 3]. The S5 axioms, the rule of necessitation, Axiom IE, and Axioms IT1 – IT4 are part of the axiomatization of Pelavin's [52] planning logic. The field axioms and the probability axioms P1, P2, and PE have appeared as parts of the axiomatization of the probability logics in [16] and [5]. The field axioms appear originally in [60].

Soundness proofs for the less commonly known axioms are given in Appendix A.

First-Order Axioms with Equality.

FOL1) $(\phi \vee \phi) \to \phi$
FOL2) $\psi \to (\phi \vee \psi)$
FOL3) $(\phi \vee \psi) \to (\psi \vee \phi)$
FOL4) $(\psi \to \gamma) \to ((\phi \vee \psi) \to (\phi \vee \gamma))$
FOL5) $\forall x \phi \to \phi(x/trm)$, where trm is substitutable[5] for x in ϕ.
EQ1) $trm=trm$, where trm is any term.
EQ2) $(trm_1 = trm_2) \to (\phi \to \phi')$, where ϕ is atomic and ϕ' is obtained by replacing trm_1 in zero or more places by trm_2.

First-Order Rules of Inference.

MoPo) Modus Ponens
   From ϕ and $\phi \to \psi$ infer ψ.
UG) Universal Generalization
   From $\phi \to \psi$ infer $\phi \to \forall x \psi$, where x does not occur free in ϕ.

---

[5] Roughly, trm is substitutable for x in ϕ if ϕ does not contain a quantifier that could capture trm.

Axioms of Real Closed Fields. These axioms capture numeric reasoning over the reals. The variables range over time points and probability values.

F1) $\forall xyz((x+y)+z = x+(y+z))$
F2) $\forall x(x+0 = x)$
F3) $\forall x(x+(-1 \cdot x) = 0)$
F4) $\forall xy(x+y = y+x)$
F5) $\forall xyz((x \cdot y) \cdot z = x \cdot (y \cdot z))$
F6) $\forall x(x \cdot 1 = x)$
F7) $\forall x(x \neq 0 \rightarrow \exists y(x \cdot y = 1))$
F8) $\forall xy(x \cdot y = y \cdot x)$
F9) $\forall xyz(x \cdot (y+z) = (x \cdot y) + (x \cdot z))$
F10) $0 \neq 1$
F11) $\forall x(\neg(x < x))$
F12) $\forall xyz((x < y) \wedge (y < z) \rightarrow (x < z))$
F13) $\forall xy((x < y) \vee (x = y) \vee (y < x))$
F14) $\forall xyz((x < y) \rightarrow ((x+z) < (y+z)))$
F15) $\forall xy(((0 < x) \wedge (0 < y)) \rightarrow (0 < x \cdot y))$
F16) $\forall x((0 < x) \rightarrow \exists y(y \cdot y = x))$
F17) Every polynomial of odd degree has a root, e.g., the axiom for a polynomial of degree 3 is

$$\forall y_0 y_1 y_2 y_3((y_0 \neq 0) \rightarrow \exists x(y_0 \cdot x \cdot x \cdot x + y_1 \cdot x \cdot x + y_2 \cdot x + y_3 = 0))$$

S5 Axioms. These axioms capture the fact that for a fixed time, inevitability is an S5 type modal operator.

I1) $\Box_t \phi \rightarrow \phi$
I2) $\Box_t(\phi \rightarrow \psi) \rightarrow (\Box_t \phi \rightarrow \Box_t \psi)$
I3) $\Box_t \phi \rightarrow \Box_t \Box_t \phi$
I4) $\Diamond_t \phi \rightarrow \Box_t \Diamond_t \phi$

Rule of Necessitation.

NEC) From ϕ conclude $\Box_t \phi$.

Probability Axioms. These axioms capture the probabilistic component of the logic. The first two axioms describe probability at a fixed time, while the third axiom describes the behavior of probability over time.

P1) Non-negativity

$$P_t(\phi) \geq 0$$

P2) Additivity

$$P_t(\phi) = P_t(\phi \wedge \psi) + P_t(\phi \wedge \neg\psi)$$

P3) Miller's principle

$$(t_1 \leq t_2) \rightarrow P_{t_1}(\phi \mid P_{t_2}(\phi) \geq \alpha) \geq \alpha$$

Axioms P1 and P2 are variants of two of the well-known three axioms of probability [39]. As mentioned earlier, variants of these axioms have appeared in [16] and [5]. Their axiomatizations also contain the third axiom of probability, represented by Fagin, et.al. as $P_t(true) = 1$ and by Bacchus as $P_t(\phi) + P_t(\neg\phi) = 1$. These axioms follow in our logic as a consequence of other axioms describing inevitability and probability. The validity of the third axiom of probability is proven as Theorem 12 in the next section.

Axiom P3 is called *Miller's principle* and several nontemporal variants of it were first suggested by Brian Skyrms [63] as possible constraints on higher-order probabilities.

Miller's principle is useful for two reasons. First, it formalizes our intuitions about the relation between chance at various times. For example, suppose that I have two coins, one fair coin and one with a 70% chance of heads and that I am going to choose one coin and flip it. What is the chance now of heads given that I will choose the biased coin? By intuition and Miller's principle it is 70%. Notice that, as Skyrms [63, Appendix 2] has pointed out, if we have a sentence in the language corresponding to the-biased-coin-is-chosen and appropriate conditional probabilities we can always represent such higher-order probability statements with simple probabilities. But we may not always have such sentences readily available.

The second useful consequence of Miller's principle is that it allows the current chance of facts and events to be inferred from the chances of their future chances: the probability at a given time is the expected value of the probability at any future time. This will be called the *expected value principle*. Suppose I am going to choose at random between the two coins above. There is a 50% chance that the chosen coin will have a 70% chance of landing heads and a 50% chance that the coin will have a 50% chance of landing heads. By Miller's principle, it follows that there is now a 60% chance that the coin flip will result in heads.

Probability of Logical Equivalents Rule. This inference rule is valid since if two sentences are logically equivalent then they hold in exactly the same possible worlds.

PE) From $\phi \leftrightarrow \psi$ infer $P_t(\phi) = P_t(\psi)$.

Temporal Logic Axioms. These axioms capture the temporal component of the logic. No specific temporal axioms are needed for reasoning about relations among time intervals since this is captured by the field axioms above.

TL1) Facts hold over their sub-intervals, except possibly at the end-points.

$$(t_1 \leq t_2 \leq t_3 \leq t_4) \wedge (t_1 \neq t_3) \wedge (t_2 \neq t_4) \rightarrow$$
$$[HOLDS(FA, t_1, t_4) \rightarrow HOLDS(FA, t_2, t_3)]$$

TL2) $HOLDS(FA, t_1, t_2) \rightarrow (t_1 \leq t_2)$
TL3) $OCCURS(EV, t_1, t_2) \rightarrow (t_1 \leq t_2)$
TL4) $OCC(A, t_1, t_2) \rightarrow (t_1 \leq t_2)$

Action Axiom. This axiom is valid since OCC is true iff both the generative and generated event tokens of the action occur, while ATT is true iff the generative event token occurs.

ACT1) $OCC(A, t_A, t'_A) \rightarrow ATT(A, t_A)$

Inevitability and Equality Axiom. This axiom is valid because the interpretation of the equality predicate is rigid across worlds.

IE) Equality is inevitable.

$$\Diamond_t(trm_1 = trm_2) \rightarrow \Box_t(trm_1 = trm_2)$$

Inevitability Temporal Axioms. This set of axioms relates the inevitability operator and the temporal component of the logic. The first axiom is valid since the set of accessible worlds becomes smaller as we move into the future. The second axiom is valid since the interpretation of relations among time points is rigid. The remaining axioms capture the intuitive property that the present and past are determined. They are valid since the inevitability operator is defined over worlds that are indistinguishable up to and including a given time.

IT1) Inevitability persists.

$$(t_1 \leq t_2) \rightarrow (\Box_{t_1} \phi \rightarrow \Box_{t_2} \phi)$$

IT2) Temporal relations are inevitable.

$$\Diamond_t(t_1 < t_2) \rightarrow \Box_t(t_1 < t_2)$$

IT3) Present and past facts are inevitable.

$$(t_1 \leq t_2) \rightarrow [\Box_{t_2} HOLDS(FA, t_0, t_1) \vee \Box_{t_2} \neg HOLDS(FA, t_0, t_1)]$$

IT4) Present and past events are inevitable.

$$(t_1 \leq t_2) \rightarrow [\Box_{t_2} OCCURS(EV, t_0, t_1) \vee \Box_{t_2} \neg OCCURS(EV, t_0, t_1)]$$

IT5) Present and past action occurrences are inevitable.

$$(t_1 \leq t_2) \rightarrow [\Box_{t_2} OCC(A, t_0, t_1) \lor \Box_{t_2} \neg OCC(A, t_0, t_1)]$$

IT6) Present and past action attempts are inevitable.

$$(t_0 \leq t_1) \rightarrow [\Box_{t_1} ATT(A, t_0) \lor \Box_{t_1} \neg ATT(A, t_0)]$$

Axioms Relating Inevitability and Probability. These axioms relate the inevitability and probability operators. Note the similarity of Axiom IP2 to the S5 axiom I4.

IP1) Inevitability implies certainty.

$$\Box_t \phi \rightarrow P_t(\phi) = 1$$

IP2) Current chance is inevitable.

$$\Diamond_t [P_t(\phi) \geq \alpha] \rightarrow \Box_t [P_t(\phi) \geq \alpha]$$

4.2   Theorems

In this section we derive several theorems that will either be useful later on or help to illustrate properties of the logic.

We first derive a few lemmas that will be used in later derivations.

Theorem 4. From $\phi \rightarrow \psi$ and $\psi \rightarrow \gamma$ infer $\phi \rightarrow \gamma$.

1. $\phi \rightarrow \psi$ Hypothesis
2. $\psi \rightarrow \gamma$ Hypothesis
3. $\neg\phi \lor \psi \rightarrow \neg\phi \lor \gamma$ FOL4: 2
4. $\psi \rightarrow \gamma$ MoPo: 1,3

Theorem 5. $\phi \rightarrow \Diamond_t \phi$

1. $\Box_t \neg\phi \rightarrow \neg\phi$ I1
2. $\Box_t \neg\phi \lor \neg\phi$ Def of $\rightarrow$
3. $\Diamond_t \phi \lor \neg\phi$ Def of $\Diamond$
4. $\phi \rightarrow \Diamond_t \phi$ Def of $\rightarrow$

Theorem 6. *From* $\phi \rightarrow \psi$ *infer* $\Box_t\phi \rightarrow \Box_t\psi$.

1. $\phi \rightarrow \psi$ Hypothesis
2. $\Box_t(\phi \rightarrow \psi)$ NEC
3. $\Box_t(\phi \rightarrow \psi) \rightarrow (\Box_t\phi \rightarrow \Box_t\psi)$ I2
4. $\Box_t\phi \rightarrow \Box_t\psi$ MoPo: 2,3

Theorem 7. $\Box_t(\phi \rightarrow \psi) \rightarrow (\Diamond_t\phi \rightarrow \Diamond_t\psi)$

1. $\Box_t(\phi \rightarrow \psi) \rightarrow \Box_t(\neg\psi \rightarrow \neg\phi)$ Def of $\rightarrow$
2. $\Box_t(\neg\psi \rightarrow \neg\phi) \rightarrow \Box_t\neg\psi \rightarrow \Box_t\neg\phi$ I2
3. $\Box_t\neg\psi \rightarrow \Box_t\neg\phi \rightarrow \Diamond_t\phi \rightarrow \Diamond_t\psi$ Def of $\rightarrow$ and $\Diamond$
4. $\Box_t(\phi \rightarrow \psi) \rightarrow (\Diamond_t\phi \rightarrow \Diamond_t\psi)$ Theorem 4: 1-3

Theorem 8. *From* $\phi \rightarrow \psi$ *infer* $\Diamond_t\phi \rightarrow \Diamond_t\psi$.

1. $\phi \rightarrow \psi$ Hypothesis
2. $\Box_t(\phi \rightarrow \psi)$ NEC
3. $\Diamond_t\phi \rightarrow \Diamond_t\psi$ Theorem 7 and MoPo

Theorem 9. $\Diamond_t(\phi \lor \psi) \rightarrow (\Diamond_t\phi \lor \Diamond_t\psi)$

1. $\Diamond_t(\phi \lor \psi) \rightarrow \neg\neg\Diamond_t(\phi \lor \psi)$ First-order axioms
2. $\neg\neg\Diamond_t(\phi \lor \psi) \rightarrow \neg\Box_t\neg(\phi \lor \psi)$ Def of $\Diamond$
3. $\neg\Box_t\neg(\phi \lor \psi) \rightarrow \neg\Box_t(\neg\phi \rightarrow \psi)$ Def of $\rightarrow$
4. $\neg\Box_t(\neg\phi \rightarrow \psi) \rightarrow \neg(\Box_t\neg\phi \rightarrow \Box_t\psi)$ I2
5. $\neg(\Box_t\neg\phi \rightarrow \Box_t\psi) \rightarrow (\neg\Box_t\neg\phi \lor \neg\Box_t\neg\psi)$ Def of $\rightarrow$
6. $(\neg\Box_t\neg\phi \lor \neg\Box_t\neg\psi) \rightarrow (\Diamond_t\phi \lor \Diamond_t\psi)$ Def of $\Diamond$
7. $\Diamond_t(\phi \lor \psi) \rightarrow (\Diamond_t\phi \lor \Diamond_t\psi)$ Theorem 4: 1-6

Theorem 10. $(\Box_t\phi \lor \Box_t\psi) \rightarrow \Box_t(\phi \lor \psi)$

1. $\phi \rightarrow (\phi \lor \psi)$ FOL2
2. $\Box_t\phi \rightarrow \Box_t(\phi \lor \psi)$ NEC, I2
3. $\psi \rightarrow (\psi \lor \phi)$ FOL2
4. $\Box_t\psi \rightarrow \Box_t(\psi \lor \phi)$ NEC, I2
5. $(\Box_t\phi \lor \Box_t\psi) \rightarrow \Box_t(\phi \lor \psi)$ First-order axioms

Field Theorems. We show the derivation of the following simple theorem to illustrate the use of the field and equality axioms. Henceforth we will simply cite the field and equality axioms to justify multiple derivation steps using them.

Theorem 11. $(trm_1 = trm_2 + s - s) \rightarrow (trm_1 = trm_2)$

1. $s + (-1 \cdot s) = 0$ F3
2. $[s + (-1 \cdot s) = 0] \rightarrow [(trm_1 = trm_2 + s - s) \rightarrow$
   $(trm_1 = trm_2 + 0)]$ EQ2
3. $(trm_1 = trm_2 + s - s) \rightarrow (trm_1 = trm_2 + 0)$ MoPo:1,2
4. $trm_2 + 0 = trm_2$ F2
5. $[trm_2 + 0 = trm_2] \rightarrow [(trm_1 = trm_2 + 0) \rightarrow (trm_1 = trm_2)]$ EQ2
6. $(trm_1 = trm_2 + 0) \rightarrow (trm_1 = trm_2)$ MoPo:4,5
7. $(trm_1 = trm_2 + s - s) \rightarrow (trm_1 = trm_2)$ MoPo:3,6

Probability Theorems. If we think of probability one as analogous to inevitability and probability greater than zero as analogous to possibility, then several of the theorems in this section can be seen as probabilistic analogues of theorems describing inevitability and possibility.

Theorem 12. *From* ϕ *infer* $P_t(\phi) = 1$

This is the third Kolmogorov axiom of probability mentioned above. It follows from properties of inevitability and the relation between probability and inevitability:

1. ϕ Hypothesis
2. $\Box_t \phi$ NEC
3. $\Box_t \phi \rightarrow P_t(\phi) = 1$ IP1
4. $P_t(\phi) = 1$ MoPo

Theorem 13. $P_t(\phi) + P_t(\neg \phi) = 1$

1. $P_t(true) = P_t(true \wedge \phi) + P_t(true \wedge \neg \phi)$ P2
2. $1 = P_t(true \wedge \phi) + P_t(true \wedge \neg \phi)$ Theorem 12, EQ2
3. $1 = P_t(\phi) + P_t(\neg \phi)$ PE, EQ2

Theorem 14. $P_t(\phi \vee \psi) = P_t(\phi) + P_t(\psi) - P_t(\phi \wedge \psi)$

1. $P_t(\phi \vee \psi) = P_t((\phi \vee \psi) \wedge \phi) + P_t((\phi \vee \psi) \wedge \neg \phi)$ P2
2. $P_t(\phi \vee \psi) = P_t(\phi) + P_t(\psi \wedge \neg \phi)$ PE, EQ2
3. $P_t(\psi) = P_t(\psi \wedge \phi) + P_t(\psi \wedge \neg \phi)$ P2
4. $P_t(\psi \wedge \neg \phi) = P_t(\psi) - P_t(\psi \wedge \phi)$ Field axioms
5. $P_t(\phi \vee \psi) = P_t(\phi) + P_t(\psi) - P_t(\psi \wedge \phi)$ EQ2

Theorem 15. *Stronger sentences have lower probability.*
From $\phi \to \psi$ infer $P_t(\phi) \leq P_t(\psi)$

1. $\phi \to \psi$ Hypothesis
2. $P_t(\phi \to \psi) = 1$ Theorem 12
3. $P_t(\neg\phi \vee \psi) = P_t(\neg\phi) + P_t(\psi) - P_t(\neg\phi \wedge \psi)$ Theorem 14
4. $1 = P_t(\neg\phi) + P_t(\psi) - P_t(\neg\phi \wedge \psi)$ PE, EQ2
5. $1 = 1 - P_t(\phi) + P_t(\psi) - P_t(\neg\phi \wedge \psi)$ Theorem 13, EQ2
6. $P_t(\phi) = P_t(\psi) - P_t(\neg\phi \wedge \psi)$ Field axioms
7. $P_t(\phi) \leq P_t(\psi)$ P1, Field axioms

Theorem 16. $P_t(\phi \wedge \psi) = P_t(\psi) \to P_t(\phi \wedge \psi \wedge \gamma) = P_t(\psi \wedge \gamma)$

1. $P_t(\psi) = P_t(\psi \wedge \gamma) + P_t(\psi \wedge \neg\gamma)$ P2
2. $P_t(\phi \wedge \psi) = P_t(\phi \wedge \psi \wedge \gamma) + P_t(\phi \wedge \psi \wedge \neg\gamma)$ P2
3. $P_t(\phi \wedge \psi) = P_t(\psi) \to$
   $P_t(\psi \wedge \gamma) + P_t(\psi \wedge \neg\gamma) =$
   $P_t(\phi \wedge \psi \wedge \gamma) + P_t(\phi \wedge \psi \wedge \neg\gamma)$ EQ2
4. $P_t(\phi \wedge \psi) = P_t(\psi) \to$
   $P_t(\psi \wedge \gamma) + P_t(\phi \wedge \psi \wedge \neg\gamma) + P_t(\neg\phi \wedge \psi \wedge \neg\gamma) =$
   $P_t(\phi \wedge \psi \wedge \gamma) + P_t(\phi \wedge \psi \wedge \neg\gamma)$ P2, EQ2
5. $P_t(\phi \wedge \psi) = P_t(\psi) \to$
   $P_t(\psi \wedge \gamma) + P_t(\neg\phi \wedge \psi \wedge \neg\gamma) = P_t(\phi \wedge \psi \wedge \gamma)$ Field axioms, EQ2
6. $P_t(\phi \wedge \psi) = P_t(\psi) \to P_t(\psi \wedge \gamma) \leq P_t(\phi \wedge \psi \wedge \gamma)$ Field axioms
7. $P_t(\psi \wedge \gamma) \geq P_t(\phi \wedge \psi \wedge \gamma)$ Theorem 15
8. $P_t(\phi \wedge \psi) = P_t(\psi) \to P_t(\psi \wedge \gamma) = P_t(\phi \wedge \psi \wedge \gamma)$ Field axioms: 6,7

Theorem 17. $P_t(\phi) = 1 \to P_t(\phi \wedge \psi) = P_t(\psi)$

1. $P_t(\phi) = P_t(\phi \wedge \psi) + P_t(\phi \wedge \neg\psi)$ P2
2. $P_t(\phi) = 1 \to 1 = P_t(\phi \wedge \psi) + P_t(\phi \wedge \neg\psi)$ EQ2
3. $P_t(\phi) = 1 \to 1 = P_t(\phi \wedge \psi) + 1 - P_t(\neg\phi \vee \psi)$ Theorem 13, EQ2
4. $P_t(\phi) = 1 \to P_t(\phi \wedge \psi) = P_t(\neg\phi \vee \psi)$ Field axioms
5. $P_t(\neg\phi \vee \psi) = P_t(\neg\phi) + P_t(\psi) - P_t(\neg\phi \wedge \psi)$ Theorem 14
6. $P_t(\neg\phi \vee \psi) = P_t(\neg\phi \wedge \psi) + P_t(\neg\phi \wedge \neg\psi) +$
   $P_t(\psi) - P_t(\neg\phi \wedge \psi)$ P2, EQ2, Field axioms
7. $P_t(\neg\phi \wedge \psi) = P_t(\psi) + P_t(\neg\phi \wedge \neg\psi)$ EQ2, Field axioms
8. $P_t(\phi) = 1 \to P_t(\phi \wedge \psi) = P_t(\psi) + P_t(\neg\phi \wedge \neg\psi)$ EQ2: 4,7
9. $P_t(\phi) = 1 \to P_t(\phi \wedge \psi) \geq P_t(\psi)$ Field axioms
10. $P_t(\phi \wedge \psi) \leq P_t(\psi)$ Theorem 15
11. $P_t(\phi) = 1 \to P_t(\phi \wedge \psi) = P_t(\psi)$ Field axioms: 9,10

Theorem 18. *Current chance is certain.*

$$P_t(\phi) \geq \alpha \;\rightarrow\; P_t(P_t(\phi) \geq \alpha) = 1$$

This is the probabilistic analogue of Axioms I3 and I4.

1. $P_t(\phi) \geq \alpha \;\rightarrow\; \Diamond_t P_t(\phi) \geq \alpha$ I1
2. $\Diamond_t P_t(\phi) \geq \alpha \;\rightarrow\; \Box_t P_t(\phi) \geq \alpha$ IP2
3. $\Box_t P_t(\phi) \geq \alpha \;\rightarrow\; P_t(P_t(\phi) \geq \alpha) = 1$ IP1
4. $P_t(\phi) \geq \alpha \;\rightarrow\; P_t(P_t(\phi) \geq \alpha) = 1$ MoPo: 1-3

Theorem 19. *Chance is the expected value of future chance.*

$$(t_1 \leq t_2) \;\rightarrow\; [P_{t_1}(P_{t_2}(\phi) \geq \alpha) \geq \beta \;\rightarrow\; P_{t_1}(\phi) \geq \alpha \cdot \beta]$$

1. $(t_1 \leq t_2) \;\rightarrow\; P_{t_1}(\phi | P_{t_2}(\phi) \geq \alpha) \geq \alpha$ P3
2. $P_{t_1}(\phi) = P_{t_1}(\phi \wedge P_{t_2}(\phi) \geq \alpha) +$
   $\qquad P_{t_1}(\phi \wedge \neg P_{t_2}(\phi) \geq \alpha)$ P2
3. $P_{t_1}(\phi) = P_{t_1}(\phi | P_{t_2}(\phi) \geq \alpha) \cdot P_{t_1}(P_{t_2}(\phi) \geq \alpha) +$
   $\qquad P_{t_1}(\phi \wedge \neg P_{t_2}(\phi) \geq \alpha)$ Def of c-prob: 2
4. $(t_1 \leq t_2) \;\rightarrow\; [P_{t_1}(P_{t_2}(\phi) \geq \alpha) \geq \beta \;\rightarrow\;$
   $\qquad P_{t_1}(\phi) \geq \alpha \cdot \beta + P_{t_1}(\phi \wedge \neg P_{t_2}(\phi) \geq \alpha)]$ Field axioms, EQ2: 1,3
5. $(t_1 \leq t_2) \;\rightarrow\; [P_{t_1}(P_{t_2}(\phi) \geq \alpha) \geq \beta \;\rightarrow\;$
   $\qquad P_{t_1}(\phi) \geq \alpha \cdot \beta]$ Field axioms

Theorem 20. *Current certainty implies certainty of future certainty.*

$$(t_1 \leq t_2) \;\rightarrow\; [P_{t_1}(\phi) = 1 \;\rightarrow\; P_{t_1}(P_{t_2}(\phi) = 1) = 1]$$

This is the probabilistic analogue of Theorem 24.

1. $P_{t_1}(\phi) = P_{t_1}(\phi \wedge P_{t_2}(\phi) = 1) +$
   $\qquad P_{t_1}(\phi \wedge P_{t_2}(\phi) < 1)$ P2
2. $(t_1 \leq t_2) \;\rightarrow\;$
   $P_{t_1}(\phi) = 1 \cdot P_{t_1}(P_{t_2}(\phi) = 1) +$
   $\qquad P_{t_1}(\phi | P_{t_2}(\phi) < 1) \cdot P_{t_1}(P_{t_2}(\phi) < 1)$ Def of c-prob, P3
3. $(t_1 \leq t_2) \;\rightarrow\;$
   $[P_{t_1}(\phi) = 1 \;\rightarrow\;$
   $1 = P_{t_1}(P_{t_2}(\phi) = 1) +$
   $\qquad P_{t_1}(\phi | P_{t_2}(\phi) < 1) \cdot P_{t_1}(P_{t_2}(\phi) < 1)]$ EQ2
4. $P_{t_1}(P_{t_2}(\phi) < 1) = 1 - P_{t_1}(P_{t_2}(\phi) = 1)$ Thrm 13
5. $(t_1 \leq t_2) \;\rightarrow\;$
   $[P_{t_1}(\phi) = 1 \;\rightarrow\;$
   $1 = P_{t_1}(\phi | P_{t_2}(\phi) < 1) +$
   $\qquad (1 - P_{t_1}(\phi | P_{t_2}(\phi) < 1)) \cdot P_{t_1}(P_{t_2}(\phi) = 1)]$ EQ2: 3,4
6. $(t_1 \leq t_2) \;\rightarrow\; P_{t_1}(\phi | P_{t_2}(\phi) < 1) < 1$ P3
7. $(t_1 \leq t_2) \;\rightarrow\; [P_{t_1}(\phi) = 1 \;\rightarrow\; P_{t_1}(P_{t_2}(\phi) = 1) = 1]$ Field axioms:5,6

Theorem 21. *Certainly later certainty implies truth.*

$$(t_1 \leq t_2) \rightarrow P_{t_1}(P_{t_2}(\phi) = 1 \rightarrow \phi) = 1$$

This is the probabilistic analogue of Axiom I1.

1.	$(t_1 \leq t_2) \rightarrow P_{t_1}(\phi | P_{t_2}(\phi) = 1) = 1$	P3
2.	$(t_1 \leq t_2) \rightarrow P_{t_1}(\phi \wedge P_{t_2}(\phi) = 1) = P_{t_1}(P_{t_2}(\phi) = 1)$	Def of c-prob

Let $A \equiv \phi$ and $B \equiv P_{t_2}(\phi) = 1$. Then

3.	$(t_1 \leq t_2) \rightarrow P_{t_1}(A \wedge B) = P_{t_1}(B)$	
4.	$P_{t_1}(B \rightarrow A) = P_{t_1}(\neg B) + P_{t_1}(A) - P_{t_1}(\neg B \wedge A)$	Theorem 14
5.	$P_{t_1}(B \rightarrow A) =$	
	$1 - P_{t_1}(B) + P_{t_1}(A) - P_{t_1}(\neg B \wedge A)$	Theorem 13
6.	$(t_1 \leq t_2) \rightarrow P_{t_1}(B \rightarrow A) = 1 - P_{t_1}(A \wedge B) +$	
	$P_{t_1}(A) - P_{t_1}(\neg B \wedge A)$	EQ2: 3,5
7.	$(t_1 \leq t_2) \rightarrow P_{t_1}(B \rightarrow A) = 1 - P_{t_1}(A) + P_{t_1}(A)$	P2, EQ2
8.	$(t_1 \leq t_2) \rightarrow P_{t_1}(B \rightarrow A) = 1$	Theorem 11
9.	$(t_1 \leq t_2) \rightarrow P_{t_1}(P_{t_2}(\phi) = 1 \rightarrow \phi) = 1$	subst. back

Theorem 22. *Certainty certainly persists.*

$$(t_0 \leq t_1 \leq t_2) \rightarrow P_{t_0}(P_{t_1}(\phi) = 1 \rightarrow P_{t_2}(\phi) = 1) = 1$$

This is the probabilistic analogue of Axiom IT1. Note that it is not valid that certainty simply persists since semantic constraint (C6) only applies to equivalence classes of worlds of positive probability.

1.	$(t_0 \leq t_1) \rightarrow P_{t_0}(P_{t_2}(\phi) = 1 | P_{t_1}(P_{t_2}(\phi) = 1) = 1) = 1$	P3
2.	$(t_0 \leq t_1) \rightarrow P_{t_0}(P_{t_2}(\phi) = 1 \wedge P_{t_1}(P_{t_2}(\phi) = 1) = 1) =$	
	$P_{t_0}(P_{t_1}(P_{t_2}(\phi) = 1) = 1)$	Def of c-prob
3.	$(t_1 \leq t_2) \rightarrow P_{t_1}(P_{t_2}(\phi) = 1) = 1 \leftrightarrow P_{t_1}(\phi) = 1$	Thrms 19 and 20
4.	$(t_0 \leq t_1 \leq t_2) \rightarrow$	
	$[P_{t_0}(P_{t_1}(P_{t_2}(\phi) = 1) = 1) = P_{t_0}(P_{t_1}(\phi) = 1)]$	PE: 3
5.	$(t_0 \leq t_1 \leq t_2) \rightarrow$	
	$[P_{t_0}(P_{t_2}(\phi) = 1 \wedge P_{t_1}(P_{t_2}(\phi) = 1) = 1) =$	
	$P_{t_0}(P_{t_1}(\phi) = 1)]$	EQ2: 2,4
6.	$(t_0 \leq t_1 \leq t_2) \rightarrow$	
	$[P_{t_0}(P_{t_2}(\phi) = 1 \wedge P_{t_1}(\phi) = 1) = P_{t_0}(P_{t_1}(\phi) = 1)]$	PE: 3,5

Letting $A \equiv P_{t_1}(\phi) = 1$ and $B \equiv P_{t_2}(\phi) = 1$, the previous line can be written as

7. $(t_0 \leq t_1 \leq t_2) \rightarrow P_{t_0}(A \wedge B) = P_{t_0}(A)$

8. $P_{t_0}(A \rightarrow B) = P_{t_0}(\neg A) + P_{t_0}(B) - P_{t_0}(\neg A \wedge B)$ Theorem 14

9. $P_{t_0}(A \rightarrow B) = 1 - P_{t_0}(A) + P_{t_0}(B) - P_{t_0}(\neg A \wedge B)$ Theorem 13

10. $(t_0 \leq t_1 \leq t_2) \rightarrow$
    $P_{t_0}(A \rightarrow B) =$
    $1 - P_{t_0}(A \wedge B) + P_{t_0}(B) - P_{t_0}(\neg A \wedge B)$ EQ2: 7,9

11. $(t_0 \leq t_1 \leq t_2) \rightarrow$
    $P_{t_0}(A \rightarrow B) = 1 - P_{t_0}(B) + P_{t_0}(B)$ P2, EQ2

12. $(t_0 \leq t_1 \leq t_2) \rightarrow P_{t_0}(A \rightarrow B) = 1$ Theorem 11

13. $(t_0 \leq t_1 \leq t_2) \rightarrow P_{t_0}(P_{t_1}(\phi) = 1 \rightarrow P_{t_2}(\phi) = 1) = 1$ substituting back

Theorem 23. *Facts have higher chance of holding over their sub-intervals.*

$$(t_1 \leq t_2 \leq t_3 \leq t_4) \wedge (t_1 \neq t_3) \wedge (t_2 \neq t_4) \rightarrow$$
$$P_t(HOLDS(FA, t_2, t_3)) \geq P_t(HOLDS(FA, t_1, t_4))$$

1. $(t_1 \leq t_2 \leq t_3 \leq t_4) \wedge (t_1 \neq t_3) \wedge (t_2 \neq t_4) \rightarrow$
   $[HOLDS(FA, t_1, t_4) \rightarrow HOLDS(FA, t_2, t_3)]$ TL1

2. $\Box_t(t_1 \leq t_2 \leq t_3 \leq t_4) \wedge (t_1 \neq t_3) \wedge (t_2 \neq t_4) \rightarrow$
   $\Box_t[HOLDS(FA, t_1, t_4) \rightarrow HOLDS(FA, t_2, t_3)]$ NEC, Theorem 6

3. $(t_1 \leq t_2 \leq t_3 \leq t_4) \wedge (t_1 \neq t_3) \wedge (t_2 \neq t_4) \rightarrow$
   $\Box_t[HOLDS(FA, t_1, t_4) \rightarrow HOLDS(FA, t_2, t_3)]$ IT2

4. $(t_1 \leq t_2 \leq t_3 \leq t_4) \wedge (t_1 \neq t_3) \wedge (t_2 \neq t_4) \rightarrow$
   $P_t(HOLDS(FA, t_1, t_4) \rightarrow HOLDS(FA, t_2, t_3)) = 1$ IP1
   The remainder of the proof follows steps 3-7 of the
   proof for Theorem 15.

Unnesting of Possibility and Inevitability. Sentences involving nested inevitability and possibility operators with arbitrary time indices may be represented by sentences with nesting only one deep. This property is formally captured by the following theorems. We provide only proofs of the first two theorems; the proofs of the remaining theorems are similar.

Theorem 24. $(t_1 \leq t_2) \rightarrow (\Box_{t_1} \Box_{t_2} \phi \leftrightarrow \Box_{t_1} \phi)$

Proof of only if part.

1. $\Box_{t_1} \Box_{t_2} \phi \rightarrow \Box_{t_2} \phi$ I1

2. $\Box_{t_2} \phi \rightarrow \phi$ I1

3. $\Box_{t_1} \Box_{t_2} \phi \rightarrow \phi$ Theorem 4: 1,2

4. $\Box_{t_1} \Box_{t_1} \Box_{t_2} \phi \rightarrow \Box_{t_1} \phi$ Theorem 6: 3

5. $\Box_{t_1}(\Box_{t_2} \phi) \rightarrow \Box_{t_1} \Box_{t_1}(\Box_{t_2} \phi)$ I3

6. $\Box_{t_1} \Box_{t_2} \phi \rightarrow \Box_{t_1} \phi$ Theorem 4: 4,5

Proof of if part.

7. $(t_1 \leq t_2) \rightarrow \Box_{t_1}\phi \rightarrow \Box_{t_2}\phi$ IT1
8. $(t_1 \leq t_2) \rightarrow \Box_{t_1}\Box_{t_1}\phi \rightarrow \Box_{t_1}\Box_{t_2}\phi$ Theorem 6, IT2
9. $\Box_{t_1}\phi \rightarrow \Box_{t_1}\Box_{t_1}\phi$ I3
10. $(t_1 \leq t_2) \rightarrow \Box_{t_1}\phi \rightarrow \Box_{t_1}\Box_{t_2}\phi$ Theorem 4: 8,9

Theorem 25. $(t_1 \leq t_2) \rightarrow (\Box_{t_2}\Box_{t_1}\phi \leftrightarrow \Box_{t_1}\phi)$

The only if part of the theorem follows directly from Axiom I1. The proof of the if part goes as follows:

1. $\Box_{t_1}\phi \rightarrow \Box_{t_1}\Box_{t_1}\phi$ I3
2. $(t_1 \leq t_2) \rightarrow (\Box_{t_1}\Box_{t_1}\phi \rightarrow \Box_{t_2}\Box_{t_1}\phi)$ IT1
3. $(t_1 \leq t_2) \rightarrow (\Box_{t_1}\phi \rightarrow \Box_{t_2}\Box_{t_1}\phi)$ Theorem 4

Theorem 26. $(t_1 \leq t_2) \rightarrow (\Diamond_{t_1}\Diamond_{t_2}\phi \leftrightarrow \Diamond_{t_1}\phi)$

Theorem 27. $(t_1 \leq t_2) \rightarrow (\Diamond_{t_2}\Diamond_{t_1}\phi \leftrightarrow \Diamond_{t_1}\phi)$

Theorem 28. $(t_1 \leq t_2) \rightarrow (\Diamond_{t_2}\Box_{t_1}\phi \leftrightarrow \Box_{t_1}\phi)$

Theorem 29. $(t_1 \leq t_2) \rightarrow (\Box_{t_2}\Diamond_{t_1}\phi \leftrightarrow \Diamond_{t_1}\phi)$

Inevitability of the Past. The first theorem is the dual of Axiom IT1 and follows trivially from it. The remaining theorems capture the semantic property that the past is determined. The proof of Theorem 31 is similar to that of Theorem 32.

Theorem 30. *Possibility persists into the past.*

$(t_1 \leq t_2) \rightarrow (\Diamond_{t_2}\phi \rightarrow \Diamond_{t_1}\phi)$

Theorem 31. *Present and past inevitability are inevitable.*

$(t_1 \leq t_2) \rightarrow (\Diamond_{t_2}\Box_{t_1}\phi \rightarrow \Box_{t_2}\Box_{t_1}\phi)$

Theorem 32. *Present and past possibility are inevitable.*

$(t_1 \leq t_2) \rightarrow (\Diamond_{t_2}\Diamond_{t_1}\phi \rightarrow \Box_{t_2}\Diamond_{t_1}\phi)$

1. $(t_1 \leq t_2) \rightarrow \Diamond_{t_2}\Diamond_{t_1}\phi \rightarrow \Diamond_{t_1}\Diamond_{t_1}\phi$ Theorem 30
2. $(t_1 \leq t_2) \rightarrow \Diamond_{t_1}\Diamond_{t_1}\phi \rightarrow \Diamond_{t_1}\phi$ Theorem 26
3. $\Diamond_{t_1}\phi \rightarrow \Box_{t_1}\Diamond_{t_1}\phi$ I4
4. $(t_1 \leq t_2) \rightarrow \Box_{t_1}\Diamond_{t_1}\phi \rightarrow \Box_{t_2}\Diamond_{t_1}\phi$ IT1
5. $(t_1 \leq t_2) \rightarrow (\Diamond_{t_2}\Diamond_{t_1}\phi \rightarrow \Box_{t_2}\Diamond_{t_1}\phi)$ Theorem 4: 1-4

Theorem 33. *Present and past chance are inevitable.*

$$(t_1 \leq t_2) \rightarrow (\Diamond_{t_2} P_{t_1}(\phi) \geq \alpha \rightarrow \Box_{t_2} P_{t_1}(\phi) \geq \alpha)$$

1. $(t_1 \leq t_2) \rightarrow \Diamond_{t_2} P_{t_1}(\phi) \geq \alpha \rightarrow \Diamond_{t_1} P_{t_1}(\phi) \geq \alpha$ Theorem 30
2. $\Diamond_{t_1} P_{t_1}(\phi) \geq \alpha \rightarrow \Box_{t_1} P_{t_1}(\phi) \geq \alpha$ IP2
3. $(t_1 \leq t_2) \rightarrow \Box_{t_1} P_{t_1}(\phi) \geq \alpha \rightarrow \Box_{t_2} P_{t_1}(\phi) \geq \alpha$ IT1
4. $(t_1 \leq t_2) \rightarrow \Diamond_{t_2} P_{t_1}(\phi) \geq \alpha \rightarrow \Box_{t_2} P_{t_1}(\phi) \geq \alpha$ Theorem 4: 1-3

Certainty of the Present and Past. By Axiom IP1 that inevitability implies certainty, the following theorems that the past is certain follow directly from the corresponding axioms and theorems for inevitability.

Theorem 34. *Present and past facts are certain.*

$$(t_1 \leq t_2) \rightarrow [P_{t_2}(HOLDS(FA, t_0, t_1)) = 1 \vee P_{t_2}(HOLDS(FA, t_0, t_1)) = 0]$$

Similar theorems hold for OCCURS, OCC, and ATT.

Theorem 35. *Present and past inevitability is certain.*

$$(t_1 \leq t_2) \rightarrow (P_{t_2}(\Box_{t_1} \phi) > 0 \rightarrow P_{t_2}(\Box_{t_1} \phi) = 1)$$

Theorem 36. *Present and past possibility is certain.*

$$(t_1 \leq t_2) \rightarrow (P_{t_2}(\Diamond_{t_1} \phi) > 0 \rightarrow P_{t_2}(\Diamond_{t_1} \phi) = 1)$$

Theorem 37. *Present and past chance is certain.*

$$(t_1 \leq t_2) \rightarrow (P_{t_2}(P_{t_1}(\phi) \geq \alpha) > 0 \rightarrow P_{t_2}(P_{t_1}(\phi) \geq \alpha) = 1)$$

Modal Operators and Quantifiers. The following theorems capture the relationships between the quantifiers and the modal operators. These theorems hold because the domain of individuals does not vary from world to world.

Theorem 38. *Barcan formula.*

$$\forall x \Box_t \phi \rightarrow \Box_t \forall x \phi, \text{ where } x \text{ does not occur free in } t.$$

1. $\forall x \Box_t \phi \rightarrow \Box_t \phi$ FOL5
2. $\Diamond_t \forall x \Box_t \phi \rightarrow \Diamond_t \Box_t \phi$ Theorem 8
3. $\Diamond_t \Box_t \phi \rightarrow \Box_t \phi$ Theorem 28
4. $\Box_t \phi \rightarrow \phi$ I1
5. $\Diamond_t \forall x \Box_t \phi \rightarrow \phi$ FOL2, MoPo
6. $\Diamond_t \forall x \Box_t \phi \rightarrow \forall x \phi$ UG
7. $\Box_t \Diamond_t \forall x \Box_t \phi \rightarrow \Box_t \forall x \phi$ Theorem 6
8. $\forall x \Box_t \phi \rightarrow \Box_t \Diamond_t \forall x \Box_t \phi$ I1, I4
9. $\forall x \Box_t \phi \rightarrow \Box_t \forall x \phi$ FOL2, MoPo

Theorem 39. *Converse Barcan formula.*

$\Box_t \forall x \phi \; \rightarrow \; \forall x \Box_t \phi$, where x does not occur free in t.

1. $\forall x \phi \rightarrow \phi$ FOL4
2. $\Box_t \forall x \phi \rightarrow \Box_t \phi$ I2, NEC
3. $\Box_t \forall x \phi \rightarrow \forall x \Box_t \phi$ UG

Theorem 40. $\Diamond_t \forall x \phi \; \rightarrow \; \forall x \Diamond_t \phi$

Theorem 41. $\exists x \Box_t \phi \; \rightarrow \; \Box_t \exists x \phi$

Theorem 42. *Probabilistic converse Barcan formula.*

$P_t(\forall x \phi) = \alpha \; \rightarrow \; \forall x P_t(\phi) \geq \alpha$

1. $\forall x \phi \rightarrow \phi$ FOL4
2. $P_t(\forall x \phi \rightarrow \phi) = 1$ Theorem 12
3. $P_t(\forall x \phi \rightarrow \phi) = 1 \; \rightarrow \; P_t(\phi \wedge \forall x \phi) = \alpha$ Theorem 17
4. $P_t(\phi \wedge \forall x \phi) = \alpha$ MoPo: 2,3
5. $P_t(\phi) \geq \alpha$ Theorem 15

Note that the probabilistic analogue of the Barcan formula $\forall x Pt(\phi) = 1 \rightarrow P_t(\forall x \phi) = 1$ is not valid because the antecedent can be satisfied by a model in which each x is true in *almost* all worlds.

Actions.

Theorem 43. *Attempted acts are feasible[6].*

$ATT(A, t_A) \rightarrow FEAS(A, t_A)$

1. $ATT(A, t_A) \rightarrow \Diamond_{t_A} ATT(A, t_A)$ Theorem 5
2. $(t \leq t_A) \rightarrow (\Diamond_{t_A} ATT(A, t_A) \rightarrow \Diamond_t ATT(A, t_A))$ Theorem 30
3. $\forall t \, (t \leq t_A) \rightarrow (\Diamond_{t_A} ATT(A, t_A) \rightarrow \Diamond_t ATT(A, t_A))$ UG
4. $\forall t \, \Diamond_{t_A} ATT(A, t_A) \rightarrow [(t \leq t_A) \rightarrow \Diamond_t ATT(A, t_A)]$ FOL axioms
5. $ATT(A, t_A) \rightarrow [\forall t \, (t \leq t_A) \rightarrow \Diamond_t ATT(A, t_A)]$ FOL axioms, MoPo
6. $ATT(A, t_A) \rightarrow FEAS(A, t_A)$ Def of *FEAS*

---

[6] The definition of feasibility is given in Sect. 5.1

Theorem 44. *Past and present feasibility is inevitable.*
$$(t_A \leq t) \rightarrow [\Diamond_t FEAS(A, t_A) \rightarrow \Box_t FEAS(A, t_A)]$$

1. $(t \leq t_0) \rightarrow [\Diamond_{t_0} \Diamond_t ATT(A, t_A) \rightarrow \Box_{t_0} \Diamond_t ATT(A, t_A)]$ Theorem 32
2. $(t_A \leq t_0) \rightarrow (t < t_A) \rightarrow (t \leq t_0)$ Field axioms
3. $(t_A \leq t_0) \rightarrow$
   $(t < t_A) \rightarrow [\Diamond_{t_0} \Diamond_t ATT(A, t_A) \rightarrow \Box_{t_0} \Diamond_t ATT(A, t_A)]$ Theorem 4: 1,2
4. $(t_A \leq t_0) \rightarrow$
   $[(t < t_A) \rightarrow \Diamond_{t_0} \Diamond_t ATT(A, t_A)] \rightarrow$
   $[(t < t_A) \rightarrow \Box_{t_0} \Diamond_t ATT(A, t_A)]$ First-order axioms

We now work on the left-hand side of sentence 4.

5. $\Diamond_{t_0}[(t < t_A) \rightarrow \Diamond_t ATT(A, t_A)] \rightarrow$
   $[\Box_{t_0}(t < t_A) \rightarrow \Diamond_{t_0} \Diamond_t ATT(A, t_A)]$ Theorem 9
6. $[\Box_{t_0}(t < t_A) \rightarrow \Diamond_{t_0} \Diamond_t ATT(A, t_A)] \rightarrow$
   $[(t < t_A) \rightarrow \Diamond_{t_0} \Diamond_t ATT(A, t_A)]$ IT1
7. $\Diamond_{t_0}[(t < t_A) \rightarrow \Diamond_t ATT(A, t_A)] \rightarrow$
   $[(t < t_A) \rightarrow \Box_{t_0} \Diamond_t ATT(A, t_A)]$ Theorem 4: 5,6

We now work on the right-hand side of sentence 7.

8. $[(t < t_A) \rightarrow \Box_{t_0} \Diamond_t ATT(A, t_A)] \rightarrow$
   $[\Diamond_{t_0}(t < t_A) \rightarrow \Box_{t_0} \Diamond_t ATT(A, t_A)]$ IT1
9. $[\Diamond_{t_0}(t < t_A) \rightarrow \Box_{t_0} \Diamond_t ATT(A, t_A)] \rightarrow$
   $\Box_{t_0}[(t < t_A) \rightarrow \Diamond_{t_0} \Diamond_t ATT(A, t_A)]$ Theorem 10
10. $\Box_{t_0}[(t < t_A) \rightarrow \Box_{t_0} \Diamond_t ATT(A, t_A)] \rightarrow$
    $\Box_{t_0}[(t < t_A) \rightarrow \Diamond_t ATT(A, t_A)]$ Theorem 29
11. $(t_A \leq t_0) \rightarrow$
    $\Diamond_{t_0}[(t < t_A) \rightarrow \Diamond_t ATT(A, t_A)] \rightarrow$
    $\Box_{t_0}[(t < t_A) \rightarrow \Diamond_t ATT(A, t_A)]$ Theorem 4: 7-10
12. $(t_A \leq t_0) \rightarrow$
    $\forall t \Diamond_{t_0}[(t < t_A) \rightarrow \Diamond_t ATT(A, t_A)] \rightarrow$
    $\forall t \Box_{t_0}[(t < t_A) \rightarrow \Diamond_t ATT(A, t_A)]$ UG
13. $(t_A \leq t_0) \rightarrow$
    $\Diamond_{t_0} FEAS(A, t_A) \rightarrow \forall t \Diamond_{t_0}[(t < t_A) \rightarrow \Diamond_t ATT(A, t_A)]$ Theorem 40,
    Def of $FEAS$
14. $\forall t \Box_{t_0}[(t < t_A) \rightarrow \Diamond_t ATT(A, t_A)] \rightarrow \Box_{t_0} FEAS(A, t_A)$ Theorem 38,
    Def of $FEAS$
15. $(t_A \leq t_0) \rightarrow [\Diamond_{t_0} FEAS(A, t_A) \rightarrow \Box_{t_0} FEAS(A, t_A)]$ MoPo

4.3 Examples

In this section two simple examples are presented to illustrate the use of the logic in reasoning about actions. The first example shows how the logic can be used to distinguish between factors that an agent cannot influence because they are inevitable and factors the agent cannot influence because they are simply independent of his available actions. Consider a game in which balls are chosen from urns. Suppose that at time t_1 I will randomly be given one of three boxes, each containing two urns. In box 1 both urns contain all red balls. In box 2 the urns contain both red and white balls and the proportions in the two urns are identical. In box 3 one urn contains all red balls and the other contains all white balls. At time t_2 I am to choose one of the urns from the box I am given and give the urn to my partner. At time t_3 she is then to choose a ball at random from that urn. What is the chance that I can influence the chance that she will draw a red ball? The situation can be described by the following sentences:

$$(now < t_1 < t_2 < t_3 < t_4) \tag{1}$$

$$P_{now}(\Box_{t_1} OCCURS(\text{red-picked}, t_3, t_4)) = 1/3 \tag{2}$$

$$P_{now}(P_{t_2}(OCCURS(\text{red-picked}, t_3, t_4)) < 1 \land$$
$$\forall x \, P_{t_2}(OCCURS(\text{red-picked}, t_3, t_4)|OCC(pick(x), t_2, t_3)) =$$
$$P_{t_2}(OCCURS(\text{red-picked}, t_3, t_4))) = 1/3 \tag{3}$$

One model in which both sentences are satisfied in all worlds is shown in figure 8.

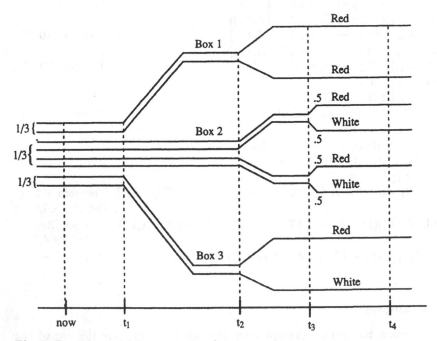

Fig. 8. Possible model for urns example.

Since inevitability persists (Axiom IT1) and stronger sentences have lower probability (Theorem 15) it follows from (2) that

$$P_{now}(\Box_{t_2}OCCURS(\text{red-picked}, t_3, t_4)) \geq 1/3 \tag{4}$$

Since inevitability implies certainty (Axiom IP1) it follows from (4) that

$$P_{now}(P_{t_2}(OCCURS(\text{red-picked}, t_3, t_4)) = 1) \geq 1/3 \tag{5}$$

By Theorem 17,

$$P_{t_2}(OCCURS(\text{red-picked}, t_3, t_4)) = 1 \rightarrow \tag{6}$$
$$P_{t_2}(OCCURS(\text{red-picked}, t_3, t_4) \land OCC(\text{pick}(x), t_2, t_3)) =$$
$$P_{t_2}(OCC(\text{pick}(x), t_2, t_3))$$

By inference rule UG and Theorem 12 it follows from (6) that

$$P_{now}(P_{t_2}(OCCURS(\text{red-picked}, t_3, t_4)) = 1 \rightarrow \tag{7}$$
$$\forall x \, P_{t_2}(OCCURS(\text{red-picked}, t_3, t_4) \land OCC(\text{pick}(x), t_2, t_3)) =$$
$$P_{t_2}(OCC(\text{pick}(x), t_2, t_3))) = 1$$

Theorem 17 applied to (5) and (7) yields

$$P_{now}(P_{t_2}(OCCURS(\text{red-picked}, t_3, t_4)) = 1 \land \tag{8}$$
$$\forall x \, P_{t_2}(OCCURS(\text{red-picked}, t_3, t_4) \land OCC(\text{pick}(x), t_2, t_3)) =$$
$$P_{t_2}(OCC(\text{pick}(x), t_2, t_3))) \geq 1/3$$

And by the definition of conditional probability,

$$P_{now}(P_{t_2}(OCCURS(\text{red-picked}, t_3, t_4)) = 1 \land \tag{9}$$
$$\forall x \, P_{t_2}(OCCURS(\text{red-picked}, t_3, t_4)|OCC(\text{pick}(x), t_2, t_3)) =$$
$$P_{t_2}(OCCURS(\text{red-picked}, t_3, t_4))) \geq 1/3$$

Finally by Axiom P2 (3) and (9) can be combined to yield

$$P_{now}(\forall x \, P_{t_2}(OCCURS(\text{red-picked}, t_3, t_4)|OCC(\text{pick}(x), t_2, t_3)) = \tag{10}$$
$$P_{t_2}(OCCURS(\text{red-picked}, t_3, t_4))) \geq 2/3$$

So there is at most a 1/3 chance that I can influence the chance of my partner picking a red ball.

The next example is a modified version of an example presented by Pelavin [52]. It illustrates how the ability of the logic to represent both probability and possibility can be used to reason about the chance that two actions can co-occur. Suppose that I am going shopping this evening and want to carry both grocery bags to the car simultaneously. In most cases it is not possible to carry two bags if it is icy out. There is a 50% chance that it will be icy out this evening. What is the chance that carrying both bags simultaneously will not be a possible course of action? The situation can be described by the following three sentences. In these sentences, the terms now, t_1, t_2, and t_3 are time constants.

$$\forall t, t' \; (now \leq t \leq t') \;\rightarrow$$
$$P_{now}(\neg \Diamond_t[OCC(\text{carry}(b1)), t, t') \wedge OCC(\text{carry}(b2)), t, t')] \mid$$
$$HOLDS(\text{icy}, t, t')) = .8 \tag{11}$$

$$P_{now}(HOLDS(\text{icy}, t_1, t_3)) = .5 \tag{12}$$

$$(now < t_1 < t_2 < t_3) \tag{13}$$

We would like to know the probability of

$$\neg \Diamond_{t_1}[OCC(\text{carry}(b1)), t_1, t_2) \wedge OCC(\text{carry}(b2)), t_1, t_2)]$$

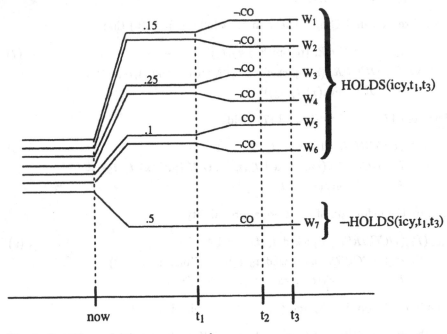

Fig. 9. Possible model for carry example.

One possible model in which the sentences are satisfied in every world is shown in Fig. 9. The labels "CO" and "¬CO" designate the co-occurrence and non co-occurrence of the two actions, respectively. Note that in worlds w_1 - w_4 we have

$$\neg \Diamond_{t_1}[OCC(\text{carry}(b1)), t_1, t_2) \wedge OCC(\text{carry}(b2)), t_1, t_2)]$$

and in w_5 and w_6 we have

$$\Diamond_{t_1}[OCC(\text{carry}(b1)), t_1, t_2) \wedge OCC(\text{carry}(b2)), t_1, t_2)].$$

The property that facts have higher chance of holding over their subintervals (Theorem 22) together with (12) and (13) entail that

$$P_{now}(HOLDS(\text{icy}, t_1, t_2)) \geq .5 \tag{14}$$

By Axiom FOL5 and MoPo it follows from (11) and (13) that

$$P_{now}(\neg \Diamond_{t_1}[OCC(\text{carry}(b1), t_1, t_2) \wedge OCC(\text{carry}(b2), t_1, t_2)] \mid$$
$$HOLDS(\text{icy}, t_1, t_2)) = .8 \tag{15}$$

By Axiom P2 it follows from (14) and (15) that

$$P_{now}(\neg \Diamond_{t_1}[OCC(\text{carry}(b1), t_1, t_2) \wedge OCC(\text{carry}(b2), t_1, t_2)]) \geq .4$$

So there is at least a 40% chance that carrying both bags simultaneously will not be possible.

Furthermore, an upper bound on the current probability of the co-occurrence of the two actions can be calculated. Since inevitability implies certainty (Axiom IP1),

$$P_{now}(P_{t_1}(OCC(\text{carry}(b1), t_1, t_2)) \wedge OCC(\text{carry}(b2), t_1, t_2)) = 0) \geq .4$$

and since chance is the expected value of future chance (Theorem 19),

$$P_{now}(OCC(\text{carry}(b1), t_1, t_2) \wedge OCC(\text{carry}(b2), t_1, t_2)) \leq .6$$

5 Properties of Actions

The representation of actions contained in our logic provides great flexibility in describing actions. We can describe actions in terms of whether they can be attempted, whether their attempt will bring about their occurrence, and what effects their attempts and occurrences will have. This next section details how actions can be described.

If an action can be attempted we say it is feasible. If an action occurs when attempted, we say that the action is executable. If an action influences the chance of certain conditions, we call these its effects. An action will be described in terms of its feasibility, its executability, and its effects.

Conditions in the world may influence the chance that an action can be attempted. For example, I can only attempt to start my car if I am at the location of the car. Such conditions are called feasibility conditions. Further conditions may influence the chance that the action will occur. For example, if I attempt to start my car I will succeed in starting it only if there is gas in the tank. Such conditions are called executability conditions. And finally conditions may influence the chance that an action will achieve certain effects. For example, if I start my car with the garage door closed there is a good chance that I will be asphyxiated. Such conditions are called ramification conditions. The following three sections discuss how $\mathcal{L}_{tca}$ can be used to describe these different aspects of actions.

5.1 Feasibility

Sometimes it may not be possible to attempt an action. This is the case if an action's generative event cannot always occur. If it is not possible to attempt an action, we say that the action is *infeasible*. Three types of infeasibility can be distinguished.

1. It may not be possible to attempt a single action under certain conditions: I cannot attempt to go from home to the office if I am not at home.
2. It may not be possible to attempt a compound action consisting to two concurrent actions under certain conditions:[7]
   I cannot attempt to drive north and drive in the direction of the wind at the same time unless the wind is blowing north.
3. A compound action consisting to two concurrent actions may not be possible to attempt under any circumstances:
   I cannot attempt to raise and lower my left arm simultaneously under any conditions.

---

[7] One could make the assumption that individual actions are always feasible but, as this example shows, once we compose actions into plans we run into the problem that the plans may not be feasible. So we may as well be completely general and not assume individual actions to be feasible.

If an action can be attempted we say that it is *feasible*.

The attempt of an action is something the agent chooses to do. As long as an action's generative event is consistent with the state of affairs of the world, the agent can choose to attempt the action and, hence, the action is feasible. *We make the simplifying assumption that an action token's generative event token is instantaneous.*[8,9] Since the agent may or may not choose to attempt an action, for an action to be feasible under this assumption it suffices that there be some action token whose generative event token is possible at an infinitesimal instant before the time of the event token. Since possibility persists into the past (Theorem 30) this can be captured by defining feasibility as possibility at all times before the time of the attempt:

Definition 45. An action A is feasible at a time t_A, written $FEAS(A, t_A)$ iff

$$\forall (t < t_A) \, \Diamond_t ATT(A, t_A).$$

This definition of feasibility seems a bit complex and two simpler alternative definitions come to mind more immediately. First, one might be tempted to define feasibility more simply as the possibility of the attempt at the time of the attempt: $\Diamond_{t_A} ATT(A, t_A)$. But because the past and present are inevitable (Axiom IT6) it follows from this that $\Box_{t_A} ATT(A, t_A)$ and this is far too strong a condition for feasibility. Second, within a probabilistic framework, a more natural definition of feasibility might seem to be $\forall (t < t_A) \, P_t(ATT(A, t_A)) > 0$. But this definition is too restrictive. In particular, it would rule out models in which there are is a uniform distribution over an uncountably infinite number of worlds and the action is attempted in only a finite number of them. In such a model, the probability of attempting the action would be zero, yet it would be possible to attempt the action.

In general, there will be a certain chance that an action is feasible – the chance that conditions in the world are consistent with the occurrence of the generative event. The chance at time t that an action A is feasible at time t_A is $P_t(FEAS(A, t_A))$. Alternatively, we can define the chance that an action is feasible as the chance that the agent succeeds in attempting the action given that

---

[8] We can think of a generative event token that spans time $t_A \, t'_A$ as a set of sequential instantaneous actions A_i. An action is then feasible if each part of the action attempt is feasible in the context of the earlier parts of the action attempt. The chance of feasibility can be represented as

$$\int_{t_A}^{t'_A} dP_t(\forall (t' < x) \, \Diamond_{t'} ATT(A_x, x) | ATT(A_{x-t_A}, t_A)) dx,$$

where $ATT(A_{x-t_A}, t_A)$ designates the occurrence of the portion of the generative event token from time t_A up to time x.

[9] Notice that had we only represented action occurrences and not attempts, we would have been forced to apply this assumption to occurrences with the result that we could not reason about actions that span time.

he tries to attempt the action, where trying to attempt an action is something the agent can always do. Trying to attempt an action can be thought of as intending or committing to attempting the action. The equivalence of this more traditional decision-theoretic notion of chance of feasibility with the above definition is shown in Appendix B. The equivalence rests on two assumptions, which can be taken as defining the properties of trying to attempt in terms of attempt and feasibility:

FA1) Trying to attempt an action results in the action's attempt if the action is feasible (in the sense of Definition 45).

FA2) The chance of feasibility of an action (in the sense of Definition 45) is independent of trying to attempt the action.

Consider again the action of starting my car and suppose that the chance that it is feasible is .8, i.e., $P_{now}(FEAS(\text{start-car}, t_A)) = .8$. One possible model for this is shown in Fig. 10. In neither world w_1 nor world w_2 does the generative event of turning the key occur. So in both w_1 and w_2 we have $\neg FEAS(\text{start-car}, t_A)$. But in worlds w_3–w_6 the attempt is possible at time t_A. So the chance that it will be within my power to choose to attempt the action is 80%.

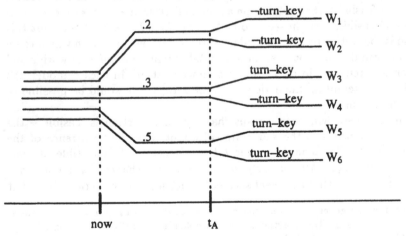

Fig. 10. Chance of feasibility.

Knowing the chance that an action is feasible provides us with information about its chance of occurrence. Suppose that for some time t

$$P_t(FEAS(A, t_A)) \leq \alpha$$

then by the relation between probability and possibility (Axiom IP1),

$$P_t(ATT(A, t_A)) \leq \alpha.$$

Since the occurrence of an action implies its attempt (Axiom 43) and stronger sentences have lower probability (Theorem 15)

$$P_t(OCC(A, t_A, t'_A)) \leq \alpha.$$

5.2 Executability

Once an agent attempts an action, whether or not the action occurs is no longer within the agent's control - it is a function of chance.

Definition 46. The chance that an action A is executable at time t_A is the chance that it occurs given that it is attempted:

$$P_t(OCC(A, t_A, t'_A) \mid ATT(A, t_A)).$$

5.3 Effects

One of the objectives of the present work is to capture some of the natural relations that exist between actions and effects. We show how various kinds of effects can be described and how some natural properties of effects follow directly from the models of chance and possibility.

An effect is a condition, the chance of which is influenced by an action. If an action increases the chance of a condition, it is called a *positive effect* and if the action decreases the chance, it is called a *negative effect*. Depending on the nature of the planning problem, we may wish to describe effects in one of two ways. If we are not concerned about the occurrence of actions, we may simply describe effects of action attempts. In this case, the chance of the effect will be represented as

$$P_t(EFF \mid ATT(A, t_A)).$$

More expressive power can be gained by describing effects of action occurrences. In this case, we distinguish between effects of a successful action and effects of a failed action. The effects of an action's occurrence are represented by an expression of the form

$$P_t(EFF \mid OCC(A, t_A, t'_A))$$

and the effects of a failed action are represented as

$$P_t(EFF \mid ATT(A, t_A) \wedge \neg \exists t'_A \, OCC(A, t_A, t'_A)).$$

We now examine what is necessary for a condition to be a positive effect of an action occurrence. Negative effects are described similarly. In describing effects we must distinguish between two cases: effects whose chance is less than one and effects whose chance equals one. The reason this distinction is necessary is that there may be a condition that has probability one of occurring, yet is not inevitable. If an action made the condition inevitable, the action would have

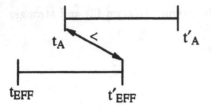

Fig. 11. Relative times of an action and its effect.

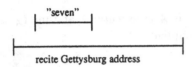

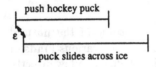

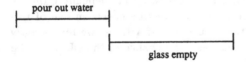

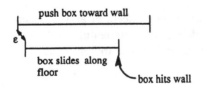

Fig. 12. Possible temporal relations between actions and effects.

positively influenced the condition and so the condition should be considered a positive effect of the action.

If the chance of *EFF* is less than one then three conditions are *necessary* for *EFF* to be a positive effect of the occurrence of an act A: [10]

1. Since actions can only influence the future, *EFF* cannot temporally precede the occurrence of A. But *EFF* need not necessarily completely succeed the occurrence of A. Figure 11 shows the necessary temporal relation between action and effect. The possible temporal relations between actions and their effects that are allowed by this constraint are shown in Fig. 12. An effect may begin before the time of an action: The action of saying the word "seven" at the right time contributes to the effect of reciting the Gettysburg address. An effect may persist after the time of an action: The effect of the hockey puck sliding across the ice persists after the action of pushing it terminates. An effect may begin exactly once the action is over: The effect of the glass being empty begins exactly once all the water is poured out. An effect may end before the action is over: The effect of the box sliding across the floor ends once it hits the wall, even though the push action is still occurring. Finally, an effect may begin some time after an action is over: The effect of the bomb exploding occurs some time after the action of setting the timer.
2. If an action has no chance of occurring at a particular time, it cannot have effects at that time. So A must have a positive chance of occurring.
3. An effect is a condition influenced by an action, so the occurrence of A must positively influence the chance of *EFF*.

If the chance of *EFF* is equal to one then four conditions are *necessary* for *EFF* to be an effect of the occurrence of an act A:

4. Again, *EFF* cannot temporally precede the occurrence of A.
5. An agent cannot influence a condition that is already inevitable, so *EFF* cannot be inevitably true.
6. Something that is not possible cannot have effects, so the occurrence of A must be possible.
7. An effect is a condition influenced by an action, so the occurrence of A must inevitably bring about *EFF*.

These two sets of conditions are fundamental properties of effects of any kind - effects of actions, effects of events, even effects of facts. They will arise again in the discussion of conditions that influence actions since the feasibility, executability, and effects of actions are in a sense effects of such conditions.

Suppose act A occurs in the interval t_A to t'_A and let *EFF* be a fact, event, or action occurrence: $HOLDS(FA, t_{EFF}, t'_{EFF})$, $OCCURS(EV, t_{EFF}, t'_{EFF})$, or $OCC(A, t_{EFF}, t'_{EFF})$. Then the conditions (i)–(vii) can be stated in the logic as

---

[10] Note that these three conditions are similar to Suppes's [66] prima facie causality conditions.

1. $P_{t_A}(EFF) < 1$ and
2. Temporal non-succession: $t_A < t'_{EFF}$
3. Positive chance of occurrence: $P_{t_A}(OCC(A, t_A, t'_A)) > 0$ [11]
4. *Positive influence:* $P_{t_A}(EFF|OCC(A, t_A, t'_A)) > P_{t_A}(EFF)$

   or

5. $P_{t_A}(EFF) = 1$ and
6. Temporal non-succession: $t_A < t'_{EFF}$
7. *Non-inevitability of effect:* $\neg\square_{t_A} EFF$
8. *Possibility of occurrence:* $\Diamond_{t_A} OCC(A, t_A, t'_A)$
9. *Inevitability of influence:* $\square_{t_A}(OCC(A, t_A, t'_A) \rightarrow EFF)$

Due to the way the semantics of $\mathcal{L}_{tca}$ has been defined, some of the above conditions entail others. It follows from the definition of objective chance that condition (4) entails conditions (1), (2), and (3). If condition (4) is expanded out into its proper form in the logic it becomes.

$$P_{t_A}(EFF \wedge OCC(A, t_A, t'_A)) > P_{t_A}(EFF) \cdot P_{t_A}(OCC(A, t_A, t'_A))$$

If condition (3) is false, i.e., $P_{t_A}(OCC(A, t_A, t'_A)) = 0$, then the above sentence is false since both sides of the inequality are zero. So if (4) holds, (3) must hold. Next, if (2) is false then $t'_{EFF} \leq t_A$. Since the present and past are certain (Theorem 34),

$$P_{t_A}(EFF) = 0 \vee P_{t_A}(EFF) = 1.$$

Either case contradicts condition (4). So if (4) holds, (2) must also hold.

Next we show that the temporal non-succession condition (6) follows from conditions (7), (8) and (9). By Theorem 7, conditions (8) and (9) together entail that

$$\Diamond_{t_A} EFF$$

which by definition is equivalent to

$$\neg\square_{t_A} \neg EFF.$$

Combining this with condition (7) we have

$$\neg(\square_{t_A} EFF \vee \square_{t_A} \neg EFF)$$

By (IT1) we have

$$(t'_{EFF} \leq t_A) \rightarrow [\square_{t_A} EFF \vee \square_{t_A} \neg EFF]$$

So it follows that

$$t_A < t'_{EFF},$$

---

[11] Note that this is equivalent to saying that the action has a positive chance of being executable,
$P_{t_A}(OCC(A, t_A, t'_A)|ATT(A, t_A)) > 0$. The equivalence follows from the fact that $P_{t_A}(OCC(A, t_A, t'_A)) > 0$ entails that $P_{t_A}(ATT(A, t_A)) > 0$.

which is exactly condition (6).

This result shows that the models have captured the natural temporal relation between actions and effects – actions can only affect future conditions. As a consequence of this result, if we use conditions (4),(7),(8), and 9) to define what is necessary for a plan to achieve a goal then actions after the time of the goal cannot contribute to achieving the goal.

The ability of the logic to represent and distinguish between truth, probability, and possibility allows us to distinguish between potential effects and actual effects. We can define actual effects as potential effects that actually occur:

$$EFF \wedge P_{t_A}(EFF|OCC(A, t_A, t'_A)) > P_{t_A}(EFF)$$

5.4 Conditions That Influence Actions

Conditions in the world may influence the feasibility, executability, and effects of actions. Such conditions are called feasibility conditions, executability conditions, and ramification conditions, respectively. In this section we present conditions, similar to those for effects, that are necessary for something to be a feasibility, executability, or ramification condition of an action.

Feasibility Conditions. Certain conditions may influence the chance that an action will be feasible. If the conditions have a positive influence they are called *positive feasibility conditions* and otherwise they are called *negative feasibility conditions*. We discuss positive feasibility conditions here; negative feasibility conditions are similar. Let FC be a fact, event, or action occurrence: $HOLDS(FA, t_{FC}, t'_{FC})$, $OCCURS(EV, t_{FC}, t'_{FC})$, or $OCC(A, t_{FC}, t'_{FC})$. As in our discussion of effects, one of two alternative sets of conditions is *necessary* for FC to be a positive feasibility condition for action A at time t_A:

1. $P_{t_{FC}}(FEAS(A, t_A)) < 1$ and
2. Temporal non-succession: $t_{FC} < t_A$
3. Positive chance of the condition: $P_{t_{FC}}(FC) > 0$
4. *Positive influence:* $P_{t_{FC}}(FEAS(A, t_A) \mid FC) > P_{t_{FC}}(FEAS(A, t_A))$
   or
5. $P_{t_{FC}}(FEAS(A, t_A)) = 1$ and
6. Temporal non-succession: $t_{FC} < t_A$
7. *Non-inevitability of feasibility:* $\neg\Box_{t_{FC}}(FEAS(A, t_A))$
8. *Possibility of condition:* $\Diamond_{t_{FC}} FC$
9. *Inevitability of influence:* $\Box_{t_{FC}}(FC \rightarrow FEAS(A, t_A))$

The temporal non-succession condition $t_{FC} < t_A$ is depicted in Fig. 13.

As was the case for action effects, condition (4) entails both conditions (2) and (3). The argument that (4) entails (3) is exactly the same as for effects. The proof that (4) entails (2) is slightly more complicated. Suppose that condition (2) is false:

1. $(t_A \leq t_{FC}) \rightarrow [\Diamond_{t_{FC}} FEAS(A, t_A) \rightarrow \Box_{t_{FC}} FEAS(A, t_A)]$ Theorem 44
2. $P_{t_{FC}}(FEAS(A, t'_A)) > 0 \rightarrow \Diamond_{t_{FC}} FEAS(A, t_A)$ IP1
3. $\Box_{t_{FC}} FEAS(A, t_A) \rightarrow P_{t_{FC}}(FEAS(A, t_A)) = 1$ IP1
4. $(t_A \leq t_{FC}) \rightarrow [P_{t_{FC}}(FEAS(A, t_A)) > 0 \rightarrow$
         $P_{t_{FC}}(FEAS(A, t_A)) = 1]$ Theorem 4: 1-3
5. $(t_A \leq t_{FC}) \rightarrow [P_{t_{FC}}(FEAS(A, t_A)) = 0 \lor$
         $P_{t_{FC}}(FEAS(A, t_A)) = 1]$ def of $\rightarrow$

Both $P_{t_{FC}}(FEAS(A, t_A)) = 0$ and $P_{t_{FC}}(FEAS(A, t_A)) = 1$ contradict condition (4). So if (4) holds, (2) must hold.

Furthermore, conditions (7), (8), and (9) entail the temporal non-succession condition (6). So again the models have captured a fundamental temporal relation: a condition that succeeds an action's attempt cannot influence the feasibility of that action.

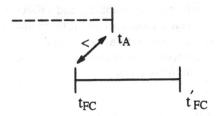

Fig. 13. Relative times of feasibility condition and action attempt.

Executability Conditions. Certain conditions may influence the chance that an action is executable. Conditions with a positive influence are called *positive executability conditions* and conditions with a negative influence are called *negative executability conditions*. Let EC be a fact, event, or action occurrence with associated interval t_{EC}, t'_{EC}. One of two alternative sets of conditions is *necessary* for EC to be a positive executability condition for action A at time t_A:

1. $P_{t_{EC}}(OCC(A, t_A, t'_A) | ATT(A, t_A)) < 1$ and
2. Temporal non-succession: $t_{EC} < t'_A$
3. Positive chance of attempt and condition: $P_{t_{EC}}(ATT(A, t_A) \land EC) > 0$
4. *Positive influence:*
    $P_{t_{EC}}(OCC(A, t_A, t'_A) | ATT(A, t_A) \land EC) >$
    $P_{t_{EC}}(OCC(A, t_A, t'_A) | ATT(A, t_A))$
    or
5. $P_{t_{EC}}(OCC(A, t_A, t'_A) | ATT(A, t_A)) = 1$ and
6. Temporal non-succession: $t_{EC} < t'_A$
7. *Non-inevitability of executability:* $\neg \Box_{t_{EC}}(ATT(A, t_A) \rightarrow OCC(A, t_A, t'_A))$
8. *Possibility of attempt and condition:* $\Diamond_{t_{EC}}(ATT(A, t_A) \land EC)$
9. *Inevitability of influence:* $\Box_{t_{EC}}(ATT(A, t_A) \land EC \rightarrow OCC(A, t_A, t'_A))$

Negative executability conditions are represented by negating the occurrence of A. Once again, condition (4) entails both conditions (2) and (3) and conditions (7), (8), and (9) entail the temporal non-succession condition (6). The proofs are similar to the earlier proofs showing that the effects of an event cannot occur prior to the time of the event.

The temporal non-succession condition $t_{EC} < t'_A$ is depicted in Fig. 14. It just says that in order for EC to influence the success of A, it cannot be a constraint on the state of the world after the time of the action. This makes good intuitive sense because executability conditions should not just provide evidence for the executability of an action but they should influence the executability. Hence, they should be worth bringing about. For example, consider a condition after the time of the action that increases the chance now that the action will be executable. Suppose that typically 15 minutes after I start my car the engine is warm:

$$P_{now}(OCC(start(car), t_1, t_2) | ATT(start(car), t_1) \wedge$$
$$\exists t_3\ HOLDS(warm(engine(car)), t_2 + 15min, t_3)) >$$
$$P_{now}(OCC(start(car), t_1, t_2) | ATT(start(car), t_1))$$

We would not want to call $\exists t_3\ HOLDS(warm(engine), t_2 + 15min, t_3)$ an executability condition for starting my car and to generate a plan to warm up my car in the future in order to make my car start now.

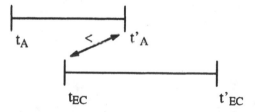

Fig. 14. Relative times of executability condition and action occurrence.

Ramification Conditions. Certain conditions in the world may influence the chance of an action's positive or negative effects. If the conditions have a positive influence on the effect, they are called *positive ramification conditions* and otherwise they are called *negative ramification conditions*. In some cases a positive ramification condition may even turn a negative effect into a positive effect, and conversely for negative ramification conditions. Let RAM be a fact, event, or action occurrence with associated interval $\langle t_{RAM}, t'_{RAM} \rangle$. Since we will primarily be concerned with the effects of the occurrences of successful actions, we will describe ramification conditions within this context. The definitions for failed actions and for simple action attempts are similar. One of two possible sets of conditions is necessary for RAM to be a positive ramification condition with respect to effect EFF for action A at time t_A:

1. $P_{t_{RAM}}(EFF \mid OCC(A, t_A, t'_A)) < 1$ and
2. *Temporal non-succession:* $t_{RAM} < t'_{EFF}$
3. *Positive chance of occurrence and condition:*
   $P_{t_{RAM}}(OCC(A, t_A, t'_A) \wedge RAM) > 0$
4. *Positive influence:*
   $P_{t_{RAM}}(EFF \mid OCC(A, t_A, t'_A) \wedge RAM) > P_{t_{RAM}}(EFF \mid OCC(A, t_A, t'_A))$
   or
5. $P_{t_{RAM}}(EFF \mid OCC(A, t_A, t'_A)) = 1$ and
6. *Temporal non-succession:* $t_{RAM} < t'_{EFF}$
7. *Non-inevitability of occurrence and condition:* $\neg \Box_{t_{RAM}}(OCC(A, t_A, t'_A) \rightarrow EFF)$
8. *Possibility of occurrence and condition:* $\Diamond_{t_{RAM}}(OCC(A, t_A, t'_A) \wedge RAM)$
9. *Inevitability of influence:* $\Box_{t_{RAM}}(OCC(A, t_A, t'_A) \wedge RAM \rightarrow EFF)$

Negative ramification conditions are represented by negating *EFF*. Condition (4) entails both conditions (2) and (3) and conditions (7), (8), and (9) entail the temporal non-succession condition (6).

The temporal relations between the action, the effect, and the ramification condition are depicted in Fig. 15. The temporal non-succession condition just says that in order for *RAM* to influence *EFF*, it cannot be a constraint on the state of the world after the time of the effect. Note, however, that *RAM* can occur after the time of the action because the effect of the action can be delayed.

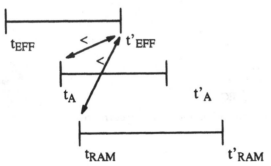

Fig. 15. Relative times an action, its effect, and ramification condition.

5.5 Properties of Plans

In general we will be interested in reasoning about plans rather than single actions. A *plan* is simply a set of actions attempted at particular times. By specifying the times of the attempts within the plan, we can represent plans containing both sequential and concurrent actions in a homogeneous manner. To reason about plans, we will simply reason about the set of actions composing them.

Feasibility of Plans. Plan feasibility is a more complex concept than action feasibility. Attempting a plan means attempting all the actions composing the plan, so a plan attempt is the conjunction of the individual action attempts. A plan is feasible if it can be attempted, i.e. if all the actions composing it can be attempted. We first examine two superficially appealing but incorrect ways of defining the chance of plan feasibility and then present a definition that has the desired intuitive properties. Consider the plan $ATT(A_1, t_{A_1}) \land ATT(A_2, t_{A_2})$, with any ordering of the attempts. First, we might be tempted to define the chance that this plan is feasible simply as the chance that each action is feasible:

$$P_t(FEAS(A_1, t_{A_1}) \land FEAS(A_2, t_{A_2}))$$

But this expression gives us too high a chance for plan feasibility because the statement $FEAS(A_1, t_{A_1}) \land FEAS(A_2, t_{A_2})$ could be satisfied by a model in which each action is attempted in some world but there is no world where they are all attempted together. Second, by analogy to action feasibility we might be tempted to define the chance that the plan is feasible as

$$P_t(\forall(t < t_{A_1}) \Diamond_t(ATT(A_1, t_{A_1}) \land ATT(A_2, t_{A_2})))$$

If $t_{A_1} = t_{A_2}$ this is the correct expression for feasibility since the joint attempt of A_1 and A_2 is equivalent to the attempt of the single more complex action. But suppose that $t_{A_1} < t_{A_2}$ and consider the model in Fig. 16. The chance of the above sentence is .8. But the chance that action A_1 is feasible is .8 while the chance that A_2 is feasible given that A_1 is attempted is only .14. So the chance that the actions composing the plan can both be attempted is only $(.8)(.14)=.11$. Hence this expression also gives us too high a value for plan feasibility.

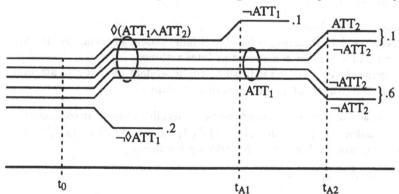

Fig. 16. Example of plan feasibility.

Each action in a plan must be feasible in the context of the attempts of the earlier actions in the plan since we wish to attempt the entire plan. So the chance that the above plan is feasible is

$$P_t(FEAS(A_2, t_{A_2}) | ATT(A_1, t_{A_1})) \cdot P_t(FEAS(A_1, t_{A_1})).$$

If $t_{A_1}=t_{A_2}$ this is also a valid expression for plan feasibility. So when $t_{A_1}=t_{A_2}$ we have

$$P_t(FEAS(A_2,t_{A_2})|ATT(A_1,t_{A_1})) \cdot P_t(FEAS(A_1,t_{A_1})) =$$
$$P_t(FEAS(\{A_1,A_2\},t_{A_1})),$$

where

$$FEAS(\{A_1,A_2\},t_{A_1}) \equiv \forall t(t<t_{A_1}) \to \Diamond_t[ATT(A_1,t_{A_1}) \wedge ATT(A_2,t_{A_2})].$$

Finally consider the plan $ATT(A_1,t_{A_1}) \wedge ATT(A_2,t_{A_2}) \wedge ATT(A_3,t_{A_3})$, where $t_{A_1} = t_{A_2}<t_{A_3}$. The chance that this plan is feasible is

$$P_t(FEAS(A_3,t_{A_3})|ATT(A_1,t_{A_1}) \wedge ATT(A_2,t_{A_2}))\cdot$$
$$P_t(FEAS(A_2,t_{A_2})|ATT(A_1,t_{A_1})) \cdot P_t(FEAS(A_1,t_{A_1}))$$

or equivalently,

$$P_t(FEAS(A_3,t_{A_3}) \mid ATT(A_1,t_{A_1}) \wedge ATT(A_2,t_{A_2}))\cdot$$
$$P_t(FEAS(\{A_1,A_2\},t_{A_1})).$$

Definition 47. In general, the chance that the plan consisting of the set of n action attempts $ATT(A_i,t_{A_i})$ with $t_{A_1}\leq t_{A_2}\leq...\leq t_{A_n}$ is feasible is

$$\prod_{i=1}^{n} P_{now}(FEAS(A_i,t_{A_i})| \wedge_{j<i} ATT(A_j,t_{A_j}))$$

In Appendix C we show how this expression can be derived using the notion of trying to attempt a plan. The derivation rests on assumption FA1 along with the additional assumptions:

FA3) Actions are volitional.

FA4) The chance that an action is feasible is independent of trying to attempt the action and any other concurrent or later actions.

FA5) The chance that an action is feasible is independent of trying to attempt the act, in the context of an earlier action attempt.

We now show that if two actions are certainly feasible then their composition is certainly feasible. Consider the plan $ATT(A_1,t_{A_1}) \wedge ATT(A_2,t_{A_2})$, where $t_{A_1}\leq t_{A_2}$ and suppose both actions are certainly feasible:

$$P_{now}(FEAS(A_1,t_{A_1})) = 1$$

$$P_{now}(FEAS(A_2,t_{A_2})) = 1$$

By the probability axioms,

$$P_{now}(FEAS(A_2,t_{A_2})|ATT(A_1,t_{A_1})) = 1$$

So the chance that the plan is feasible is

$$P_{now}(FEAS(A_2,t_{A_2})|ATT(A_1,t_{A_1})) \cdot P_{now}(FEAS(A_1,t_{A_1})) = 1$$

Executability of Plans. The chance that a plan is executable is represented by an expression of the form

$$P_t(\wedge_i OCC(A_i, t_{Ai}, t'_{Ai})| \wedge_i ATT(A_i, t_{Ai})).$$

Just as with individual actions, plans may have executability conditions.

Effects of Plans. The chance of the effect of a successful plan is represented by an expression of the form

$$P_t(EFF| \wedge_i OCC(A_i, t_{Ai}, t'_{Ai})).$$

Effects of plan attempts and of failed plans are represented similarly.

5.6 Conditional Probability vs Probability of Implication

In a probability logic, one can think of representing the probabilistic influence of one sentence on another in at least two ways: with conditional probability and with the probability of a material implication. In representing the effects of actions and events, as well as the executability of. actions, we have exclusively chosen to use conditional probability. There is good reason for this.

Consider two sentences ϕ and ψ. The conditional probability sentence $P_t(\phi|\psi) = \alpha$ is true if the probability of the worlds in which $\phi \wedge \psi$ is true relative to the probability of those in which ψ is true is α. This essentially says that the chance of ϕ given that we are in the set of worlds in which ψ is true is α. On the other hand, $P_t(\psi \rightarrow \phi) = \alpha$ is true if the probability of the set of worlds in which ψ is false or ϕ is true is α. So, while the conditional probability is a measure of the relevance of the truth of ψ to the probability of ϕ, the probability of the material implication, is a measure of not only the probability of the worlds in which ϕ and ψ are true but also of the probability of the worlds in which ψ is false. But if we are interested in the influence of ψ on ϕ, the set of worlds in which ψ is false is irrelevant. When reasoning about the effects of actions and events we are interested in what the chance of the effect would be if the action or event were to occur. To evaluate such a subjunctive conditional we are only interested in worlds where the antecedent is true.

An extreme example will help to illustrate the point. Suppose that ϕ and ψ are mutually exclusive so that $P_t(\phi) = .01$, $P_t(\psi) = .5$, and $P_t(\phi \wedge \psi) = 0$. Then $P_t(\phi|\psi) = 0$ but $P_t(\psi \rightarrow \phi) = .99$. Clearly conditional probability more accurately captures the relationship between ϕ and ψ in this situation than does the probability of the material implication. In fact, the probability of the material implication is always at least as high as that of the conditional probability. The proof goes as follows:

1. $P_t(\phi \wedge \psi) \leq P_t(\psi)$ Theorem 15
2. $P_t(\phi \wedge \psi) \cdot P_t(\neg\psi) \leq P_t(\psi) \cdot P_t(\neg\psi)$ Field axioms
3. $P_t(\phi \wedge \psi) - P_t(\phi \wedge \psi) \cdot P_t(\psi) \leq$
   $P_t(\psi) \cdot P_t(\neg\psi)$ Theorem 13
4. $P_t(\psi \wedge \psi) \leq P_t(\psi)(P_t(\phi \wedge \psi) + P_t(\neg\psi))$ Field axioms
5. $P_t(\phi|\psi) \leq P_t(\psi \rightarrow \phi)$ Def of c-prob, Theorem 14

It is also worth mentioning that $P_t(\phi|\psi) = 1$ if and only if $P_t(\psi \rightarrow \phi) = 1$.

6 Goals and Utilities

6.1 Expected Utility of Actions

Earlier we mentioned that one of the primary motivations for using a decision theoretic framework to reason about plans is the link that it provides between the problem representation and the concept of rationality. Decision theory tells us that if an agent's preferences are represented in terms of probabilities and utilities then that agent's choices are rational just in case they correspond to those alternatives that maximize expected utility. So to draw upon the decision theoretic notion of rationality, we must provide a notion of expected utility for the present framework.

The present work departs from classical decision-theoretic representations of actions in two ways:

1. We distinguish action attempts from action occurrences.
2. We do not assume that actions are feasible.

The first point is not fundamental since action attempts can be treated as simple actions and the occurrences can be thought of as consequences of action attempts. The second distinction does represent a fundamental departure from classical Decision Theory.

Decision Theory has traditionally assumed that it is always within the agent's power to perform an act. So all acts are assumed to be feasible. We compare our representation of actions with the two predominant formulations of Subjective Decision Theory, that of Savage[58] and of Jeffrey[35]. In Savage's decision theory, an act is a function from states to outcomes. Since the action functions are assumed to be defined for all states, actions are always feasible, i.e. can be executed in any state and have a well-defined outcome.[12] The expected utility of an action A is then simply defined as:[13]

$$\mathbf{SEU}(A) = \sum_{s \in S} P(s) \cdot u(A(s)),$$

where s is a state and $u(A(s))$ is the utility of the outcome that results from performing action A in state s.

In Jeffrey's decision theory, an action is simply a proposition, i.e., a set of states. It is assumed that the agent can always make the proposition representing the action true. In other words, it is assumed that it is always within the agent's power to raise the probability of the action to one. Consequently, the conditional expected utility of an act A is defined as:

$$\mathbf{CEU}(A) = \sum_{s \in S} P(s|A) \cdot u(s),$$

---

[12] Hanks[31] extends Savage's definition of actions to allow for actions that may not be executable by defining a null outcome into which an action maps a state in which it is undefined.

[13] For simplicity of exposition, we use a discrete sums rather than integrals throughout this chapter.

where s is a state and $u(s)$ is the utility of that state.

Our treatment of actions is similar to Jeffrey's in that action attempts can be taken to represent a set of worlds – the worlds in which the attempt predicate is true. But since we no longer assume it is always within the agent's power to make the expression representing the action attempt true, we must calculate the expected utility of *trying* to attempt the action. In the definition below, $TATT(A, t_A)$ denotes trying to attempt action A at time t_A, i.e. committing to $ATT(A, t_A)$.

Definition 48. The expected utility at time t of trying to attempt act A at time t_A is

$$\mathbf{EUT}(ATT(A, t_A), t) = \sum_{w \in W} [P_t(w|ATT(A, t_A)) \cdot P_t(FEAS(A, t_A)) + \quad (16)$$
$$P_t(w|\neg FEAS(A, t_A) \wedge TATT(A, t_A)) \cdot$$
$$P_t(\neg FEAS(A, t_A))] \cdot \mathbf{U}(w)$$

Note that in worlds where the action is feasible, we condition on the attempt of the action because in these worlds we can choose to attempt the action. In worlds where the action is not feasible, we condition on trying to attempt the act and the lack of feasibility of the act. In Appendix D we show how this expression can be derived using Jeffrey's definition of expected utility and the notion of trying to attempt an action. The derivation depends on the three assumptions FA1), FA2), and FA3) described earlier.

When the action is certainly feasible, the expression for **EUT** reduces to simple conditional expected utility:

$$\mathbf{EUT}(ATT(A, t_A), t) = \sum_{w_i \in W} P_t(w_i|ATT(A, t_A)) \cdot \mathbf{U}(w_i)$$

An example will help illustrate why, when an action may not be feasible, the expected utility of trying to attempt the action is not simply the conditional expected utility of attempting the act. Consider the model shown in Fig. 17. In worlds w_1–w_3 the act is now feasible and in worlds w_4–w_5 it is not. The conditional expected utility of attempting the act in each world w may be written as

$$\mathbf{CEU}(ATT(A, t_A), now) = \sum_{w_i \in W} P_{now}(w_i|ATT(A, t_A)) \cdot \mathbf{U}(w_i)$$
$$= (.08/.09)(1) + (.01/.09)(0)$$
$$= .89$$

But the current probability that the act is feasible is quite low

$$P_{now}(FEAS(A, t_A)) = .1$$

So the expected utility of trying to attempt A in each world w is

$$\mathbf{EUT}(ATT(A, t_A), now) = (.08/.09)(.1)(1) + (.01/.09)(.1)(0) + (.3)(1)$$
$$= .389$$

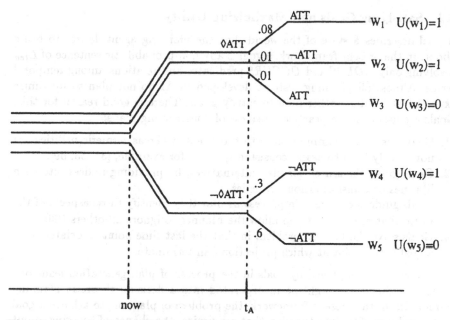

Fig. 17. Example of a possibly infeasible action.

which is much lower than the conditional expected utility. When choosing among actions that may not be feasible, **EUT** is the correct form of expected utility to use.

Some work in Decision Theory has addressed the the problem of actions that may not be feasible. Dummett [14] touches on the issue by describing an action as being "reasonable for an agent to perform" if among other things, "it is within his power to perform it."

Sobel [65] studies some of the implications for Bayesian Decision Theory of considering acts that may not be feasible. He takes actions to be propositions and defines a proposition to be open for an agent iff it is true or the agent can make the proposition true. He defines the expected utility of an act A as

$$\mathbf{EU(A)} = \sum_{\mathbf{w} \in (\mathbf{A})} \frac{P[\Diamond A \wedge (A \Box\!\!\rightarrow w)]}{P(\Diamond A)} \mathbf{V(w)},$$

where P is the agent's subjective probability, $\Diamond A$ means that A is open, $\Box\!\!\rightarrow$ is a counterfactual operator, and $V(w)$ is the utility of world w. This expression represents the effects of action A in those worlds in which it is feasible. So Sobel is representing the expected utility of actually bringing about action A while we are describing the expected utility of trying to bring about action A. Sobel's approach differs further from ours in that he does not formalize the notion of being open in terms of an underlying model theory, he does not address temporal aspects of decision, and he carries out his analysis only for deterministic acts, i.e. "for agents who do not believe in objective chance."

6.2 Satisfying Goals and Maximizing Utility

A goal describes a state of the world that the planning agent desires to bring about. In the present framework, a goal is any non-probabilistic sentence of $\mathcal{L}_{tca}$ involving only $HOLDS$ and $OCCURS$ predicates and relations among temporal terms. Almost all planning systems developed in AI do not plan to maximize expected utility but rather plan to satisfy goals. There is good reason for this. Goals are useful in the practical business of constructing plans:

1. Goals are easily communicated to the agent, whereas numeric utilities are notoriously hard to assess consistently—see, for example, [38, 33, 59].
2. Goals guide the search for plan alternatives, by providing indices into plan libraries or transformation strategies.
3. Goals guide the projection process in that they identify those aspects of the world that are relevant and allow the planner to ignore all others ([30]).
4. Goals solve the horizon problem in that the last time point associated with a goal is the point at which projection can terminate.

The crucial role played by goals in the process of plan generation leads one to ask whether they might be incorporated into a decision theoretic planning framework. In the present framework, the problem of planning to achieve a goal is the problem of finding the plan that maximizes the chance of bringing about the goal. So we might ask, for what forms of utility functions does choosing the plan that maximizes the probability of the goal lead to choosing the plan that maximizes expected utility? The answer is that this relationship holds only for simple step utility functions, functions for which utility is a constant low value for outcomes in which the goal is not satisfied and a constant high value for outcomes in which the goal is satisfied. Such a function is shown in Fig. 18. Utility is represented along the vertical axis and the space of possible world-histories along the horizontal axis. G and $\overline{G}$ designate the set of all worlds that satisfy and do not satisfy the goal, respectively.

To demonstrate this fact we first provide the following theorem. By substituting the indicator function of a sentence ϕ for $U(w)$ in the expression for **EUT** (Definition 48), we obtain an expression for the chance that trying to attempt an action brings about the sentence ϕ.

Theorem 49. *For any act A_i with associated attempt $ATT(A_i, t_i)$ and feasibility $FEAS(A_i, t_i)$ and any sentence ϕ the chance that trying to attempt act A_i brings about ϕ is*

$$p_i(\phi) = P_{now}(\phi|ATT(A_i, t_i)) \cdot P_{now}(FEAS(A_i, t_i)) + \tag{17}$$
$$P_{now}(\phi|\neg FEAS(A_i, t_i) \wedge TATT(A_i, t_i)) \cdot P_{now}(\neg FEAS(A_i, t_i))$$

Theorem 50. *Let $p_1(G)$ and $p_2(G)$ denote the chance the trying to attempt action A_1 and trying to attempt action A_2 achieves goal G, respectively. If $p_1(G) \geq p_2(G)$ then $\mathbf{EUT}(A_1) \geq \mathbf{EUT}(A_2)$ for all actions A_1 and A_2 if and only if the utility function U is such that i) $U(w_i) \geq U(w_j)$ whenever w_i satisfies G and w_j falsifies G, and ii) $U(w_i) = U(w_j)$ whenever w_i and w_j both satisfy or both falsify G.*

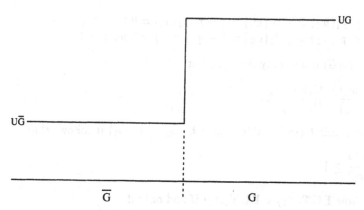

Fig. 18. Step utility function.

Proof. We first show that this form of the utility function is a sufficient condition for $p_1(G) \geq p_2(G)$ to imply that $\mathbf{EUT}(A_1) \geq \mathbf{EUT}(A_2)$ for all actions A_1 and A_2. Suppose that $p_1(G) \geq p_2(G)$ and that we have two constants, UG and $\mathsf{U\overline{G}}$ such that $\mathsf{UG} \geq \mathsf{U\overline{G}}$. Then by algebraic identity

$$(\mathsf{UG} - \mathsf{U\overline{G}}) \cdot p_1(G) + \mathsf{U\overline{G}} \geq (\mathsf{UG} - \mathsf{U\overline{G}}) \cdot p_2(G) + \mathsf{U\overline{G}}.$$

Rearranging terms,

$$\mathsf{UG} \cdot p_1(G) + \mathsf{U\overline{G}}(1 - p_1(G)) \geq \mathsf{UG} \cdot p_2(G) + \mathsf{U\overline{G}}(1 - p_2(G))$$

So if UG represents the utility associated with satisfying the goal and $\mathsf{U\overline{G}}$ represents the utility associated with failing to do so, then $\mathbf{EUT}(A_1) \geq \mathbf{EUT}(A_2)$.

Next we show that the utility function must necessarily take the form of a step function for $p_1(G) \geq p_2(G)$ to imply that $\mathbf{EUT}(A_1) \geq \mathbf{EUT}(A_2)$ for all actions A_1 and A_2. We first show that if condition *(i)* does not hold then we may have $p_1(G) \geq p_2(G)$ but $\mathbf{EUT}(A_1) < \mathbf{EUT}(A_2)$. Consider a model with at least two worlds w_1 and w_2 with $\mathbf{U}(w_1) < \mathbf{U}(w_2)$. Suppose that we have the following probabilities associated with the two actions

$A_1: p_1(w_1) = 1, p_1(w_2) = 0, p_1(w_i) = 0$ for $i > 2$ and
$A_2: p_2(w_1) = 0, p_2(w_2) = 1, p_2(w_i) = 0$ for $i > 2$,

and suppose that G is satisifed by w_1 but not by w_2. Then $p_1(G) \geq p_2(G)$ but since $\mathbf{EUT}(A_1) = \mathbf{U}(w_1)$ and $\mathbf{EUT}(A_2) = \mathbf{U}(w_2)$, $\mathbf{EUT}(A_1) < \mathbf{EUT}(A_2)$.

Now we show that if condition *(ii)* does not hold then we may have $p_1(G) \geq p_2(G)$ but $\mathbf{EUT}(A_1) < \mathbf{EUT}(A_2)$. Consider a model with at least three worlds w_1, w_2, and w_3. Let w_1 and w_2 be two worlds that satisfy G and let U be a utility function that assigns different utilities to these two worlds. Assume without loss of generality that $\mathbf{U}(w_1) < \mathbf{U}(w_2)$. Let w_3 be a world that does not satisfy the goal. Consider the following two actions:

A_1: $p_1(w_1) = p$, $p_1(w_2) = 0$, $p_1(w_3) = 1 - p$, $p_1(w_i) = 0$ for $i > 3$
A_2: $p_2(w_1) = 0$, $p_2(w_2) = q$, $p_2(w_3) = 1 - q$, $p_2(w_i) = 0$ for $i > 3$

Note that $p_1(G) \geq p_2(G)$ if and only if $p \geq q$. Let

$$p = \left(q + q \frac{\mathbf{U}(w_2) - \mathbf{U}(w_3)}{\mathbf{U}(w_1) - \mathbf{U}(w_3)} \right) / 2.$$

Since by the above result $\mathbf{U}(w_3) \leq \mathbf{U}(w_1)$ and $\mathbf{U}(w_3) \leq \mathbf{U}(w_2)$ it follows that

$$\frac{\mathbf{U}(w_2) - \mathbf{U}(w_3)}{\mathbf{U}(w_1) - \mathbf{U}(w_3)} \geq 1$$

and hence $p \geq q$. Now $\mathbf{EUT}(A_1) < \mathbf{EUT}(A_2)$ if and only if

$$p\mathbf{U}(w_1) + (1 - p)\mathbf{U}(w_3) < q\mathbf{U}(w_2) + (1 - q)\mathbf{U}(w_3).$$

Rearranging terms we have

$$p < q \frac{\mathbf{U}(w_2) - \mathbf{U}(w_3)}{\mathbf{U}(w_1) - \mathbf{U}(w_3)}.$$

Since

$$\left(q + q \frac{\mathbf{U}(w_2) - \mathbf{U}(w_3)}{\mathbf{U}(w_1) - \mathbf{U}(w_3)} \right) / 2 < q \frac{\mathbf{U}(w_2) - \mathbf{U}(w_3)}{\mathbf{U}(w_1) - \mathbf{U}(w_3)}$$

we have $\mathbf{EUT}(A_1) < \mathbf{EUT}(A_2)$. This argument can be duplicated for the negation of the goal. □

In practice, few utility functions actually take the form of such a simple step function. Utility is likely not to be perfectly flat over any region, and it may contain continuous transitions rather than discontinuities. In the next three sections we discuss how to handle these cases.

Noise in the Step Function. What can be said if the utility function has the discontinuity of a step function but is not otherwise constant? Suppose that we have a discontinuous utility function such that the worlds that satisfy the goal all have relatively high utility and those that do not all have relatively low utility as shown in Fig. 19. $\mathbf{U\overline{G}}_L$ and $\mathbf{U\overline{G}}_H$ are the lowest and highest utility for worlds that do not satisfy the goal. $\mathbf{UG}_L$ and $\mathbf{UG}_H$ are the lowest and highest utility for worlds that satisfy the goal. Suppose we are considering two plans A_1 and A_2 with probabilities of achieving the goal $p_1(G)$ and $p_2(G)$, respectively. For what values of $p_1(G)$ and $p_2(G)$ can we say that plan A_1 is preferred to plan A_2? Since we don't know the exact outcomes of the plans, we must do a worst-case analysis. The lowest possible expected utility for A_1 is $p_1(G) \cdot \mathbf{UG}_L + (1 - p_1(G)) \cdot \mathbf{U\overline{G}}_L$. The highest possible expected utility for A_2 is $p_2(G) \cdot \mathbf{UG}_H + (1 - p_2(G)) \cdot \mathbf{U\overline{G}}_H$. A_1 is guaranteed to be preferred to A_2 just in case

$$p_1(G) \cdot \mathbf{UG}_L + (1 - p_1(G)) \cdot \mathbf{U\overline{G}}_L > p_2(G) \cdot \mathbf{UG}_H + (1 - p_2(G)) \cdot \mathbf{U\overline{G}}_H.$$

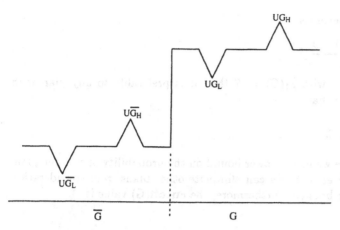

Fig. 19. Noisy step utility function.

Rearranging terms,

$$(UG_L - U\overline{G}_L)p_1(G) + U\overline{G}_L > (UG_H - U\overline{G}_H)p_2(G) + U\overline{G}_H$$

and finally

$$p_1(G) > \frac{(UG_H - U\overline{G}_H)p_2(G) + (U\overline{G}_H - U\overline{G}_L)}{UG_L - U\overline{G}_L}. \tag{18}$$

By comparing probabilities in this way we can eliminate the set of plans known to be sub-optimal and use more refined methods (e.g. complete expected utility calculation) to identify the best plan among the candidates left. (Note the similarity to [73].) Furthermore, if we substitute probability 1 for $p_1(G)$ we can see that any plan with probability greater than

$$\textbf{cutoff}(G) = \frac{(UG_L - U\overline{G}_H)}{(UG_H - U\overline{G}_H)}$$

is guaranteed to be in the candidate set (that is, among the set of non-dominated plans). The reason is that no plan can have a probability of achieving the goal greater than one, so there can be no plan with probability of achieving the goal high enough to be preferred to any plan that has probability of achieving the goal at least as great as the cutoff value. In order to compare plans in terms of their probability of achieving the goal using inequality (18), we need not calculate precise point probability values. It is sufficient to establish upper and lower bounds on the probabilities. This can result in computational savings (see, for example, [31, 23, 20]).

A simple numerical example will help to illustrate how these results can be used. Suppose that

$$U\overline{G}_L = -13 \qquad U\overline{G}_H = -4 \qquad UG_L = +8 \qquad UG_H = +15.$$

Then inequality 18 becomes

$$p_1(G) > \frac{19p_2(G) + 9}{21}$$

If we have a plan A_1 with $p_1(G) = .7$ then it is preferable to any plan with probability $p_2(G)$ less than

$$\frac{(.7)(21) - 9}{19} = 0.3$$

This means that once we have a lower bound on the probability of any one plan, if this bound is high enough, we can eliminate other plans from consideration based on their upper bounds. Furthermore, the **cutoff**(G) value is

$$\frac{8 + 4}{15 + 4} = 0.63,$$

so any plan with a probability of achieving the goal of at least 0.63 is guaranteed to be in the candidate set.

Any plan that is related to *all others* by inequality (18) is guaranteed to be one that maximizes utility. What if there is no such plan? We can still quantify the degree of approximation involved in choosing the plan that has the highest probability of achieving the goal. Suppose the two plans with highest probability of achieving the goal are A_1 and A_2 and that $p_1(G) > p_2(G)$. But suppose that A_2 actually has a higher expected utility than A_1. To what degree does choosing A_1 approximate maximizing expected utility? (In other words, how far wrong can we go by choosing A_1?) This degree of approximation can be expressed as the percent that A_1 falls short of maximizing expected utility. In the worst case, $\mathbf{EUT}(A_1) = p_1(G) \cdot \mathrm{UG}_L + (1 - p_1(G)) \cdot \overline{\mathrm{UG}}_L$ and $\mathbf{EUT}(A_2) = p_2(G) \cdot \mathrm{UG}_H + (1 - p_2(G)) \cdot \mathrm{UG}_H$. The worst-case degree of approximation can then be defined as:

$$\frac{\mathbf{EUT}(A_2) - \mathbf{EUT}(A_1)}{\mathbf{EUT}(A_2)}.$$

In the previous example, if $p_1(G) = .7$ and $p_2(G) = .35$, the degree of approximation in choosing A_1 is

$$\frac{[.35(15) + .6(-4)] - [.7(8) + .3(-13)]}{.35(15) + .6(-4)} = .40$$

So at best A_1 is the act that maximizes expected utility and at worst its expected utility is 60% that of the best plan.

Non-step Utility Functions. Suppose now that the utility function has the two flat regions characteristic of a step function but the transition between these regions is not a single discontinuity. Figure 20 shows the graph of a univariate utility function that is continuous in the value of the attribute variable. The utility function can be qualitatively described by specifying the three distinct regions of the space of worlds over which it is flat, transitionary, and flat again. If we have a symbolic description of each of these regions, plans can be described in terms of their probability of achieving an outcome that satisfies each of the descriptions $p_i(X_i)$, where X_i is one of the utility regions as in Fig. 20.

Suppose we are considering two plans A_1 and A_2 with probability distributions $p_1(\cdot)$ and $p_2(\cdot)$, respectively. For what sorts of distributions $p_1(\cdot)$ and $p_2(\cdot)$ can we say that A_1 is preferred to A_2?

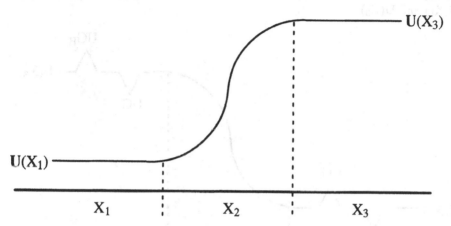

Fig. 20. Non-step utility function.

The lowest possible expected utility for A_1 is

$$p_1(X_3) \cdot U(X_3) + (1 - p_1(X_3)) \cdot U(X_1),$$

and the highest possible expected utility for A_2 is

$$p_2(X_1) \cdot U(X_1) + (1 - p_2(X_1)) \cdot U(X_3).$$

A_1 is therefore guaranteed to be preferred to A_2 just in case

$$p_1(X_3) \cdot U(X_3) + (1 - p_1(X_3)) \cdot U(X_1) >$$
$$p_2(X_1) \cdot U(X_1) + (1 - p_2(X_1)) \cdot U(X_3)$$

$$p_1(X_3) \cdot (U(X_3) - U(X_1)) + U(X_1) >$$
$$p_2(X_1) \cdot (U(X_1) - U(X_3)) + U(X_3)$$

$$p_1(X_3) > \frac{p_2(X_1) \cdot (U(X_1) - U(X_3)) + (U(X_3) - U(X_1))}{(U(X_3) - U(X_1))}$$

and finally

$$p_1(X_3) > 1 - p_2(X_1). \tag{19}$$

Notice that the utility values no longer appear in the inequality.

The smaller the X_2 region, the easier inequality (19) is to satisfy. If $p_1(X_2) = p_2(X_2) = 0$ then 19 reduces to the simple step function condition

$$p_1(X_3) > p_2(X_3).$$

Inequality 19 holds not only for the utility function shown in the figure but for any utility function in which the utilities of worlds in region X_2 are between $U(X_1)$ and $U(X_3)$.

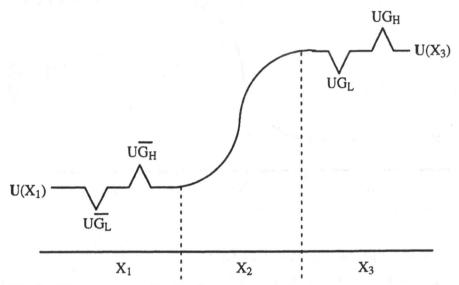

Fig. 21. Noisy non-step utility function.

Non-step Utility Functions With Noise. Now suppose we have a non-step utility function with noise as shown in Fig. 21. Suppose that $U\overline{G}_L$ is the lowest utility in the X_2 region as well as the X_1 region, and that UG_H is the highest utility in the X_2 region as well as the X_3 region. Then plan A_1 is guaranteed to be preferable to plan A_2 just in case

$$p_1(X_3) \cdot UG_L + (1 - p_1(X_3)) \cdot U\overline{G}_L >$$
$$p_2(X_1) \cdot U\overline{G}_H + (1 - p_2(X_1)) \cdot UG_H$$

which simplifies to

$$p_1(X_3) > \frac{p_2(X_1) \cdot (U\overline{G}_H - UG_H) + (UG_H - U\overline{G}_L)}{(UG_L - U\overline{G}_L)}. \tag{20}$$

The four forms of utility functions just analyzed are not the only possible forms one might consider. They are prototypical examples of how, by generalizing the notion of goal and relating it to utilities, goals can be used to characterize more general preference structures.

Under the strict definition of goal (which has been a standard for AI), a goal is a logical expression that describes two regions of the outcome space: the region in which the goal is satisfied and the one where it is not. The set of worlds that satisfy the goal have constant high utility and the set of worlds that falsify the goal have constant low utility. We have shown how the concept of goal can be generalized. Under our new, more general definition, a goal describes a partition of the set of possible worlds such that within each region of the partition, all utility values fall within given bounds. The strict definition of goal is the degenerate case, in which there are only two partitions and the upper and lower bounds in each region of the partition are equal.

In the remainder of the monograph, we will show how planning problems can be represented in $\mathcal{L}_{tca}$ in such a way that we can reason about bounds on the chance that a plan achieves a given goal, where it is understood that the goal represents a region of bounded utility in the sense described above.

7 Describing and Reasoning About Planning Problems

In this chapter we present a general framework for describing planning problems. The purpose of the framework is to provide guidance in the use of the rich language of $\mathcal{L}_{tca}$. The main purpose of describing planning problems is to use the description in the generation and evaluation of plans. So in developing the framework, we focus on descriptions that are compositional, in the sense that properties of a plan may be inferred from the properties of the component actions and the environment. We present one way in which $\mathcal{L}_{tca}$ can be used to specify such a description. Many alternatives are possible.

7.1 Representing the Planning Problem

In this section we show how $\mathcal{L}_{tca}$ can be used to describe planning problems so that we can reason about the chance that a plan will achieve a given goal. Since the best knowledge we have about chance is the chance now, in describing the planning problem all probabilities will be taken relative to the present time. A planning problem is described in terms of (i) the planning environment, (ii) the individual action specifications, (iii) the action interactions, and (iv) the goal description. Following Pelavin [52], we call the world within which planning takes place the planning environment. Since we are working in a temporal setting, the description of the planning environment can include chances of facts and events that hold or occur at any time. The individual action specifications describe feasibility conditions, executability conditions, and effects with associated ramification conditions for each action. Although in principle the goal description may be any sentence of $\mathcal{L}_{tca}$, in practice we restrict the goal description to be any non-probabilistic sentence of $\mathcal{L}_{tca}$ involving only $HOLDS$ and $OCCURS$ predicates and temporal relations. Since we are primarily concerned with reasoning about probabilities, we will assume henceforth that goals currently hold with probability less than one. So the planning description will be assumed to contain a sentence of the form $P_{now}(\text{Goal}) < 1$. Due to the potential complex nature of action interactions in the present framework, the description of action interactions will be specific to a given planning problem and is discussed in section 7.2.

Throughout this chapter, will be concerned with deriving a lower bound on the chance that a plan achieves a goal. So it will suffice to specify lower bounds on all probability values.

The Planning Environment. The planning environment is described in terms of the chances that facts hold and events occur:

$P_{now}(HOLDS(FA, t_{\mathrm{F}}, t_{\mathrm{F}}')) \geq \alpha$

$P_{now}(OCCURS(EV, t_{\mathrm{E}}, t_{\mathrm{E}}')) \geq \alpha$

as well as temporal constraints relating the times of facts and events:

$(now < t_{\mathrm{F}} \leq t_{\mathrm{E}})$

Feasibility Conditions. Action feasibility conditions FC are described by sentences of the form

$$P_{now}(FEAS(A, t_A)|FC) \geq \alpha,$$

where t_{FC} is the earliest time associated with FC and $t_{FC} < t_A$.

Feasibility conditions can be used to represent interference between actions. The following sentence says that action A_2 is not feasible as long as A_1 is being performed.

$$P_{now}(FEAS(A_2, t_{A_2})|OCC(A_1, t_{A_1}, t'_{A_1}) \wedge (t_{A_1} \leq t_{A_2} \leq t'_{A_1})) = 0$$

Executability Conditions. Executability conditions EC are described by sentences of the form

$$P_{now}(OCC(A, t_A, t'_A)|ATT(A, t_A) \wedge EC) \geq \alpha, \tag{21}$$

where the earliest time associated with EC is t_{EC}, and $t_{EC} < t'_A$. Executability conditions are assumed to be independent of the action with which they are associated:

IA1) $P_{now}(EC \mid ATT(A, t_A)) = P_{now}(EC)$

So a lower bound for the chance that the action is executable can be expressed in terms of the executability specification (21) and the chance of the executability condition:

$$P_{now}(OCC(A, t_A, t'_A) \mid ATT(A, t_A)) \geq$$
$$P_{now}(OCC(A, t_A, t'_A) \mid ATT(A, t_A) \wedge EC) \cdot P_{now}(EC)$$

Assumption IA1 reduces the complexity of inference and is reasonable in most cases.

Effects and Ramification Conditions. We describe positive action effects by sentences of the form:

$$P_{now}(EFF|OCC(A, t_A, t'_A) \wedge RAM) \geq \alpha \tag{22}$$

where RAM represents the ramification conditions for effect EFF of action A, the latest times associated with EFF is t_{EFF}, the earliest time associated with RAM is t_{RAM}, and $t_{RAM} < t'_{EFF}$. Ramification conditions are assumed to be independent of the action with which they are associated:

IA2) $P_{now}(RAM \mid OCC(A, t_A, t'_A)) = P_{now}(RAM)$

So a lower bound for the chance of the action's positive effects can be expressed in terms of the positive effect specification (22) and the chance of the ramification condition:

$$P_{now}(EFF \mid OCC(A, t_A, t'_A)) \geq$$
$$P_{now}(EFF \mid OCC(A, t_A, t'_A) \wedge RAM) \cdot P_{now}(RAM)$$

The Goal Description. The goal description is any non-probabilistic sentence of $\mathcal{L}_{tca}$ involving only $HOLDS$ and $OCCURS$ predicates and temporal relations. For example, the goal of getting to the bank by 5:00pm may be represented as

$$\exists t_1, t_2 \, (t_1 < 5{:}00) \wedge HOLDS(\text{loc}(\text{me,bank}), t_1, t_2).$$

The Probability of Goal Achievement. In order to compare alternative plans, we will be interested in inferring the chance that trying to attempt a given plan achieves a given goal. For a plan with n action attempts such that $t_{A_1} \le t_{A_2} \le ... \le t_{A_n}$ a lower bound on the chance that trying to attempt the plan achieves goal G is the chance that the attempt of the plan brings about the goal multiplied by the chance that the plan is feasible:

$$P_{now}(G| \bigwedge_{i=1}^{n} ATT(A_i, t_{A_i})) \cdot \prod_{i=1}^{n} P_{now}(FEAS(A_i, t_{A_i})| \bigwedge_{j<i} ATT(A_j, t_{A_j}))(23)$$

This is only a lower bound since the goal may come about even if some of the actions are not attempted.

If the failed attempt of a plan does not influence the chance of our goal, we can focus on the chance that trying to attempt a plan achieves both the occurrence of the plan and the goal. This is just the chance that the plan attempt brings about both the plan occurrence and the goal multiplied by the chance that the plan is feasible:

$$P_{now}(G \wedge_i OCC(A_i, t_{A_i}, t'_{A_i})| \wedge_i ATT(A_i, t_{A_i})) \cdot \qquad (24)$$
$$\prod_{i=1}^{n} P_{now}(FEAS(A_i, t_{A_i})| \bigwedge_{j<i} ATT(A_j, t_{A_j}))$$

Note that this is a lower bound on the chance that trying to attempt the plan brings about the goal. In Appendix E expressions (23) and (24) are derived using the notion of trying to attempt a plan.

Inferring the Probability of a Goal from Action Specifications. Describing the feasibility, executability, and effects of actions is only useful for planning purposes if these descriptions can be combined to infer the chance that a plan will achieve a given goal. We show here how these descriptions can be combined to infer the chance that attempting a single action will result in the action occurring and in a given goal being achieved. For plans consisting of multiple actions we need additional information concerning the interactions of the actions composing the plan. Since numerous types of action interactions are possible, we will give specific examples later of performing such inference for more complex plans.

Suppose we wish to achieve goal G and suppose that G is an effect of action A. The chance that trying to attempt A results in A occurring and achieves G is

$$P_{now}(G \wedge OCC(A, t_A, t'_A) \mid ATT(A, t_A)) \cdot P_{now}(FEAS(A, t_A))$$

By the definition of c-prob the first term can be written as

$$P_{now}(G \wedge OCC(A, t_A, t'_A) \mid ATT(A, t_A)) =$$
$$P_{now}(G \mid OCC(A, t_A, t'_A) \wedge ATT(A, t_A)) \cdot$$
$$P_{now}(OCC(A, t_A, t'_A) \mid ATT(A, t_A))$$

By Axiom ACT1,

$$P_{now}(G \mid OCC(A, t_A, t'_A) \wedge ATT(A, t_A)) = P_{now}(G \mid OCC(A, t_A, t'_A))$$

So the chance of achieving goal G can be expressed in terms of the feasibility, executability, and effects of A:

$$P_{now}(G \wedge OCC(A, t_A, t'_A) \mid ATT(A, t_A)) \cdot P_{now}(FEAS(A, t_A)) =$$
$$P_{now}(G \mid OCC(A, t_A, t'_A)) \cdot P_{now}(OCC(A, t_A, t'_A) \mid ATT(A, t_A)) \cdot$$
$$P_{now}(FEAS(A, t_A))$$

If action A has ramification, executability, and feasibility conditions associated with it then by independence assumptions IA1 and IA2 we have

$$P_{now}(G \wedge OCC(A, t_A, t'_A) \mid ATT(A, t_A)) \cdot P_{now}(FEAS(A, t_A)) \geq$$
$$P_{now}(G \mid OCC(A, t_A, t'_A) \wedge RAM) \cdot$$
$$P_{now}(OCC(A, t_A, t'_A) \mid ATT(A, t_A) \wedge EC) \cdot$$
$$P_{now}(FEAS(A, t_A) \mid FC) \cdot P_{now}(RAM) \cdot P_{now}(EC) \cdot P_{now}(FC)$$

7.2 Elaborations of the Basic Framework

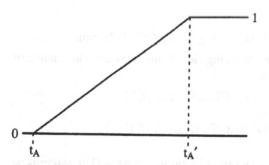

Fig. 22. Uniform cumulative distribution function.

Action Duration. Actions will not always take a fixed amount of time to perform. There may be uncertainty associated with the time required to complete an action once it is attempted. This can be represented using a cumulative distribution function. The following sentence says that if action A is attempted at time t_A the chance that it will be completed by time t' is represented by the cumulative distribution function (cdf) of the uniform distribution over the interval t_A to t'_A. The distribution is shown in Fig. 22.

$$\forall t' \, P_{now}(\exists t \, (t \leq t') \wedge OCC(A, t_A, t) \mid ATT(A, t_A)) = u(t', t_A, t'_A)$$

Resource Availability. Often an action must wait for a certain condition to hold or for an event to occur and there may be uncertainty associated with the time the fact becomes true or the event occurs. For example, resource procurement typically requires a certain lead time - procuring steel members may require 6 to 8 weeks. The exact amount of lead time is typically uncertain and the uncertainty often conforms to a beta distribution. Feasibility conditions can be used to represent the dependence between the timing of an action and resource procurement lead time:

$$\forall t' \, P_{now}(\exists t \, (t \leq t') \land HOLDS(\text{avail(steel)}, t, 100)) = \text{Beta}(t', \alpha, \beta)$$

$$P_{now}(FEAS(\text{install(frame)}, t_A) \,|$$
$$\exists t_1 \, (t_1 \leq t_A) \land HOLDS(\text{avail(steel)}, t_1, t_2)) = 1$$

It follows from these two sentences that the chance of feasibility of installing the steel frame at different times is a beta distribution with parameters α and β.

Conditions Influenced by Actions and Events. In a deterministic setting a condition is either influenced or not influenced by an action or event. But in the present probabilistic framework, we can distinguish finer degrees of influence such as conditions that an action can only positively influence, conditions an action can only negatively influence, and conditions that are independent of an action. There are five different types of probabilistic influence constraints, corresponding to each of the possible numerical relationships: $<, \leq, =, \geq, >$. For example, we can represent the sentence, "The chance of rain is independent of my clapping my hands." as

$$\forall t, t_1, t_2, t_3, t_4 \, (t_1 \leq t_3) \, \rightarrow$$
$$P_t(OCCURS(\text{rain}, t_3, t_4) | OCC(\text{clap}, t_1, t_2)) = P_t(OCCURS(\text{rain}, t_3, t_4))$$

And we can represent the sentence, "Seeding the clouds increases the chance of having rain within the next day." as

$$P_{now}(\exists t_r, t'_r \, (t'_s \leq t_r \leq t'_s + 1\text{day}) \land OCCURS(\text{rain}, t_r, t'_r) \,|$$
$$OCC(\text{seed-clouds}, t_s, t'_s)) >$$
$$P_{now}(\exists t_r, t'_r \, (t'_s \leq t_r \leq t'_s + 1\text{day}) \land OCCURS(\text{rain}, t_r, t'_r))$$

Action Interactions. Actions may interact in numerous ways. The attempt or occurrence of one action may positively or negatively influence another action's feasibility, executability, or effects. Some interactions are desirable while some are not. Typically, a positive influence of one action A_1 on the feasibility or executability of another action A_2 is desirable. If it were undesirable, we would not consider including A_2 in our plan. The desirability of the interactions between one action's attempt or occurrence and another action's effects depends on the context of the planning problem. For example the occurrence of one action may decrease the chance of another action's positive effect. If the effect is desired, the interaction may be detrimental. But if the effect is some negative side effect we wish to suppress, then the interaction may be beneficial. We give examples of how several different types of action interaction may be represented.

Mutually Reinforcing Concurrent Actions. Actions may beneficially interact by reinforcing one another's desired effects. This is the special case in which a positive ramification condition for one action is the occurrence of another action and in which the relationship is symmetric with respect to both actions. Suppose I am driving my car and I wish to throw it into a spin. If I hit the brakes there is a slight chance the car will spin:

$$\forall t_1, t_2 \, (t_1 > now) \rightarrow P_{now}(\exists t_3, t_4 \, (t_1 < t_3 \leq t_2) \wedge OCCURS(\text{spin}, t_3, t_4) \mid$$
$$OCC(\text{hit-brakes}, t_1, t_2)) = .2$$

If I turn the wheel sharply there is a better chance the car will spin:

$$\forall t_1, t_2 \, (t_1 > now) \rightarrow P_{now}(\exists t_3, t_4 \, (t_1 < t_3 \leq t_2) \wedge OCCURS(\text{spin}, t_3, t_4) \mid$$
$$OCC(\text{turn-wheel}, t_1, t_2)) = .5$$

But if I do both concurrently there is a very good chance the car will spin:

$$\forall t_1, t_2 \, (t_1 > now) \rightarrow$$
$$P_{now}(\exists t_3, t_4 \, (t_1 < t_3 \leq t_2) \wedge OCCURS(\text{spin}, t_3, t_4) \mid$$
$$OCC(\text{hit-brakes}, t_1, t_2) \wedge OCC(\text{turn-wheel}, t_1, t_2)) = .8$$

So the concurrent execution of the two actions reinforces the same desired effect of each.

Interference with Feasibility. One action may interfere with another action's feasibility in numerous ways. One of the more common types of such interference is the competition of two or more actions for some limited resource. In resource competition the interference is mutual – if insufficient resources are available, neither action can be attempted while the other is being performed. In typical warehouse construction, for example, both roof trusses and wall panels are installed using a crane.[14] If only one crane is available, each activity cannot be attempted while the other is being performed:

$$\forall t_r, t_w, t_w' \, P_{now}(FEAS(\text{install(roof-trusses)}, t_r) \mid \qquad (25)$$
$$OCC(\text{install(wall-panels)}, t_w, t_w') \wedge (t_r < t_w') \wedge$$
$$\exists t \, (t < t_r) \wedge HOLDS((\text{number(cranes)} \leq 1), t, t_r)) = 0$$

$$\forall t_w, t_r, t_r' \, P_{now}(FEAS(\text{install(wall-panels)}, t_w) \mid \qquad (26)$$
$$OCC(\text{install(roof-trusses)}, t_r, t_r') \wedge (t_w < t_r') \wedge$$
$$\exists t \, (t < t_w) \wedge HOLDS((\text{number(cranes)} \leq 1), t, t_r)) = 0$$

Suppose we have the following time line

$$(t_1 < t_2 < t_3)$$

---

[14] This and the following two examples are taken from Echeverry's [15] analysis of the construction scheduling task.

and suppose there is a 70% chance we will have only one crane available

$$P_{now}(HOLDS((\text{number(cranes)}=1), t_1, t_3)) = .7 \tag{27}$$

Then it follows from (25) and (27) by Axiom FOL5 and the definition of c-prob that there is at most a 30% chance we can attempt to install the roof trusses while the wall panels are being installed.

$$P_{now}(FEAS(\text{install(roof-trusses)}, t_2) \mid OCC(\text{install(wall-panels)}, t_1, t_3)) \leq .3$$

Interference with Executability. Sometimes two actions can interfere with one another in such a way that they do not prevent each other from occurring but simply delay each other's completion. This situation arises in the construction planning domain when two actions compete for space. For example, painting the walls in a room and laying the carpet may occur concurrently but the two crews are likely to interfere with one another. Suppose that the time required to complete painting the walls is

$$\forall t' \, P_{now}(\exists t_1 \, (t_1 \leq t') \land OCC(\text{paint(walls)}, t_A, t_1) \mid ATT(\text{paint(walls)}, t_A)) = u(t', t_A, t_A + 3)$$

and the time required to install the carpet is

$$\forall t' \, P_{now}(\exists t_2 \, (t_2 \leq t') \land OCC(\text{install(carpet)}, t_A, t_2) \mid \\ ATT(\text{install(carpet)}, t_A)) = u(t', t_A, t_A + 4)$$

Suppose further that the chance that both activities are completed by a given time is represented by the cumulative distribution function of the uniform distribution from t_A to $t_A + 5$:

$$\forall t' \, P_{now}(\exists t_1, t_2 \, (t_1 \leq t') \land (t_2 \leq t') \land \\ OCC(\text{paint(walls)}, t_A, t_1) \land OCC(\text{install(carpet)}, t_A, t_2) \mid \\ ATT(\text{paint(walls)}, t_A) \land ATT(\text{install(carpet)}, t_A)) = u(t', t_A, t_A + 5)$$

Note that A_1 and A_2 need not be attempted concurrently for them to interfere with one another. They would still interfere if they just overlapped in time.

Then the time required to guarantee completion of painting the walls if the activities are performed concurrently is 5 days and the same holds for installing the carpet. The time required to guarantee completion if the activities are performed sequentially is 3 days for painting the walls and 4 days for installing the carpet. So performing the actions concurrently will result in earlier completion but the total time spent on both activities if performed concurrently is 10 days while that spent if performed sequentially is only 7 days. If cost is proportional to time spent on an activity then in this case sequential execution would be the less costly alternative.

Interference with Effects One action may interfere with another action in such a way that the concurrent execution of the two actions results in undesirable side effects. For example, in typical steel frame construction fireproofing is sprayed onto the frame. This process produces a hazardous environment and if any other work crews are present in the area the chance of their being injured is high. Let fireproofing(x,z) denote the action of crew x fireproofing room z and rough-in-work(y,z) denote the action of crew y doing the rough-in work on room z. Then the situation can be represented as follows. The chance that someone will be injured during the fireproofing if the fireproofing is being done alone is quite low:

$$\forall t_1, t_2, x, z \, P_{now}(\exists t_3, t_4, y \, (t_1 \leq t_3 \leq t_4 \leq t_2) \wedge OCCURS(\text{injury}(y), t_3, t_4) \mid$$
$$OCC(\text{fireproofing}(x,z), t_1, t_2)) \leq .01$$

But if one crew is doing the rough-in work on a room while another crew is spraying the fireproofing, the chance of the first getting injured is at least 70%:

$$\forall t_1, t_2, x, y, z$$
$$P_{now}(\exists t_3, t_4 \, (t_1 \leq t_3 \leq t_4 \leq t_2) \wedge OCCURS(\text{injury}(y), t_3, t_4) \mid$$
$$OCC(\text{fireproofing}(x,z), t_1, t_2) \wedge OCC(\text{rough-in-work}(y,z), t_1, t_2)) \geq .7$$

Notice that the occurrence of the rough-in work functions as a positive ramification condition because its presence increases the chance of the undesirable effect of an injury.

8 Planning Example

This section presents a detailed example of the use of the representational framework in reasoning about plans. Suppose I am at home and would like to go to my favorite restaurant for dinner. The restaurant does not take reservations. Under normal circumstances, I can get a table within fifteen minutes but if a theater performance has ended in the last hour, the wait could be much longer. We would like to determine the chance that the plan consisting of starting my car and driving to the restaurant will result in having dinner without having to wait too long. A further complication is that my car is fairly unreliable and is only likely to start if the temperature is above freezing. The problem is described by specifying the feasibility, executability, and effects for the two actions, the interactions between the actions, the state of the planning environment, and the desired goal.

Start(car) Executability: I can usually start my car if the temperature is above freezing while I am trying to start it.

$$\forall t_s \, (t_s > now) \rightarrow \tag{28}$$
$$P_{now}(OCC(\text{start}(car), t_s, t_s + 1) \mid$$
$$ATT(\text{start}(car), t_s) \wedge HOLDS((temp > 32), t_s, t_s + 1)) \geq .95$$

Feasibility: I can attempt to start my car if I have the keys and am at the same location as the car.

$$\forall t_s, t', x \, (t_s > now) \rightarrow \tag{29}$$
$$P_{now}(FEAS(\text{start(car)}, t_s) \mid HOLDS(\text{have(keys)}, t', t_s) \land$$
$$HOLDS(\text{loc(me,x)}, t', t_s) \land HOLDS(\text{loc(car,x)}, t', t_s)) = 1$$

Drive(home,restaurant) Effects: There is at least an 80% chance that if I drive to the restaurant I will get a table within 15 minutes, as long as no theater performance ended within an hour of my arrival at the restaurant.

$$\forall t_d, t'_d \, P_{now}(\exists t, t' \, (t'_d \leq t \leq t'_d + 15) \land OCCURS(\text{get(table)}, t, t') \mid \tag{30}$$
$$OCC(\text{drive(home,restaurant)}, t_d, t'_d) \land$$
$$\neg \exists t_p, t'_p \, (t'_p < t'_d \leq t'_p + 60) \land OCCURS(\text{performance}, t_p, t'_p)) \geq .8$$

Executability: I can successfully drive to the restaurant if I can first start my car. Notice that the executability condition is the occurrence of the action of starting my car.

$$\forall t, t_d \, (t_d > now) \rightarrow \tag{31}$$
$$P_{now}(OCC(\text{drive(home,restaurant)}, t_d, t_d + 10) \mid$$
$$ATT(\text{drive(home,restaurant)}, t_d) \land OCC(\text{start(car)}, t, t_d)) = 1$$

Feasibility: I can attempt to drive from home to the restaurant if both I and my car are at home.
$$\forall t, t_d \, (t_d > now) \rightarrow \tag{32}$$
$$P_{now}(FEAS(\text{drive(home,restaurant)}, t_d) \mid$$
$$HOLDS(\text{loc(me,home)}, t, t_d) \land HOLDS(\text{loc(car,home)}, t, t_d)) = 1$$

Action Interactions We assume that the actions of starting the car and driving to the restaurant do not negatively influence one another. This is represented by the following three sentences. Attempting to start the car does not negatively influence the feasibility of driving the car at a later time.

$$\forall t_d, t_s, x, y \, (t_s < t_d) \rightarrow \tag{33}$$
$$P_{now}(FEAS(\text{drive(x,y)}, t_d) \mid ATT(\text{start(car)}, t_s)) \geq$$
$$P_{now}(FEAS(\text{drive(x,y)}, t_d))$$

Starting the car does not negatively influence the effects of driving to the restaurant at a later time.

$$\forall t_d, t'_d, t_s, t'_s \, (t'_s \leq t_d) \rightarrow \tag{34}$$
$$P_{now}(\exists t, t' \, (t'_d \leq t \leq t'_d + 15) \land OCCURS(\text{get(table)}, t, t') \mid$$
$$OCC(\text{drive(home,restaurant)}, t_d, t'_d) \land OCC(\text{start(car)}, t_s, t'_s)) \geq$$
$$P_{now}(\exists t, t' \, (t'_d \leq t \leq t'_d + 15) \land OCCURS(\text{get(table)}, t, t') \mid$$
$$OCC(\text{drive(home,restaurant)}, t_d, t'_d))$$

Attempting to drive to the restaurant does not negatively influence the executability of starting the car at an earlier time.

$$\forall t_d, t_s, t_s' \, (t_s' \leq t_d) \rightarrow \tag{35}$$
$$P_{now}(OCC(\text{start(car)}, t_s, t_s') \mid$$
$$\quad ATT(\text{start(car)}, t_s) \wedge ATT(\text{drive(home,restaurant)}, t_d)) \geq$$
$$P_{now}(OCC(\text{start(car)}, t_s, t_s') \mid ATT(\text{start(car)}, t_s))$$

Planning Environment We have the following time line.

$$(now < t_0 < t_1) \tag{36}$$

There is an 80% the temperature will be above freezing this evening.

$$P_{now}(HOLDS((\text{temp} > 32), t_1, t_1 + 120)) = .8 \tag{37}$$

I am certain to have my keys this evening.

$$P_{now}(HOLDS(\text{have(keys)}, t_0, t_1)) = 1 \tag{38}$$

I am certain to be at home this evening.[15]

$$P_{now}(HOLDS(\text{loc(me,home)}, t_0, t_1 + 1)) = 1 \tag{39}$$

My car is likely to be at home this evening.

$$P_{now}(HOLDS(\text{loc(car,home)}, t_0, t_1 + 1)) \geq .95 \tag{40}$$

There is no theater performance this evening.

$$P_{now}(\exists t, t' \, (t' \leq t_1 + 120) \wedge OCCURS(\text{performance}, t, t')) = 0 \tag{41}$$

Goal My goal is to get a table within thirty minutes of t_1.

$$\exists t_G, t_G' \, (t_1 < t_G \leq t_1 + 30) \wedge OCCURS(\text{get(table)}, t_G, t_G')$$

---

[15] Since my location is essentially within my control, this would more accurately be represented with a stay-at-location action:

$$\forall x, n, t \, P_{now}(OCC(\text{stay(x,n)}, t, t + n) \mid ATT(\text{stay(x,n)}, t)) = 1$$

$$\forall x, n, t \, P_{now}(HOLDS(\text{loc(me,x)}, t, t + n) \mid OCC(\text{stay(x,n)}, t, t + n)) = 1,$$

where stay(x,n) means that I stay at location x for n time units. For simplicity of exposition we have omitted this action from the plan.

The Derivation We want to derive the chance that the plan consisting of starting my car at time t_1 and driving to the restaurant at time $t_1 + 1$ will occur and achieve the goal:

$$P_{now}(\exists t_G, t'_G \, (t_G \leq t_1 + 30) \wedge OCCURS(\text{get(table)}, t_G, t'_G) \wedge \qquad (42)$$
$$OCC(\text{drive(home,restaurant)}, t_1 + 1, t_1 + 11) \wedge$$
$$OCC(\text{start(car)}, t_1, t_1 + 1) \mid$$
$$ATT(\text{drive(home,restaurant)}, t_1 + 1) \wedge ATT(\text{start(car)}, t_1)) \cdot$$
$$P_{now}(FEAS(\text{drive(home,restaurant)}, t_1 + 1) \mid ATT(\text{start(car)}, t_1)) \cdot \qquad (43)$$
$$P_{now}(FEAS(\text{start(car)}, t_1)) \qquad (44)$$

We calculate a lower bound on the chance of each of the terms (42), (43), and (44).

Calculation of (44) By Axiom FOL5 and (29),

$$P_{now}(FEAS(\text{start(car)}, t_1) \mid HOLDS(\text{have(keys)}, t_0, t_1) \wedge \qquad (45)$$
$$HOLDS(\text{loc(me,home)}, t_0, t_1) \wedge HOLDS(\text{loc(car,home)}, t_0, t_1)) = 1$$

By Theorem 17 and (38), (39), and (40) it follows that

$$P_{now}(HOLDS(\text{have(keys)}, t_0, t_1) \wedge HOLDS(\text{loc(me,home)}, t_0, t_1) \wedge \qquad (46)$$
$$HOLDS(\text{loc(car,home)}, t_0, t_1)) \geq .95$$

By the definition of c-prob and Theorem 15 applied to (45) and (46),

$$P_{now}(FEAS(\text{start(car)}, t_1)) \geq .95 \qquad (47)$$

Calculation of (43) By Axiom FOL5 and (32),

$$P_{now}(FEAS(\text{drive(home,restaurant)}, t_1 + 1) \mid \qquad (48)$$
$$HOLDS(\text{loc(me,home)}, t_0, t_1 + 1) \wedge$$
$$HOLDS(\text{loc(car,home)}, t_0, t_1 + 1)) = 1$$

By Theorem 17 and (39) and (40),

$$P_{now}(HOLDS(\text{loc(me,home)}, t_0, t_1 + 1) \wedge \qquad (49)$$
$$HOLDS(\text{loc(car,home)}, t_0, t_1 + 1)) \geq .95$$

By the definition of c-prob and Theorem 15 applied to (48) and (49),

$$P_{now}(FEAS(\text{drive(home,restaurant)}, t_1 + 1)) \geq .95 \qquad (50)$$

By FOL5 and the field axioms applied to (50) and (33),

$$P_{now}(FEAS(\text{drive(home,restaurant)}, t_1 + 1) \mid ATT(\text{start(car)}, t_1)) \geq .95 \quad (51)$$

Calculation of (42) By the definition of c-prob and Axiom ACT1, term (42) may be rewritten as

$P_{now}(\exists t_G, t_G' \, (t_G \leq t_1 + 30) \wedge OCCURS(\text{get(table)}, t_G, t_G') \wedge$
$\quad OCC(\text{drive(home,restaurant)}, t_1 + 1, t_1 + 11) \wedge$
$\quad OCC(\text{start(car)}, t_1, t_1 + 1) \,|$
$\quad ATT(\text{drive(home,restaurant)}, t_1 + 1) \wedge ATT(\text{start(car)}, t_1)) =$

$P_{now}(\exists t_G, t_G' \, (t_G \leq t_1 + 30) \wedge OCCURS(\text{get(table)}, t_G, t_G') \,| \qquad (52)$
$\quad OCC(\text{drive(home,restaurant)}, t_1 + 1, t_1 + 11) \wedge$
$\quad OCC(\text{start(car)}, t_1, t_1 + 1)) \cdot$

$P_{now}(OCC(\text{drive(home,restaurant)}, t_1 + 1, t_1 + 11) \wedge \qquad (53)$
$\quad OCC(\text{start(car)}, t_1, t_1 + 1) \,|$
$\quad ATT(\text{drive(home,restaurant)}, t_1 + 1) \wedge ATT(\text{start(car)}, t_1))$

Since $(t_1 + 11 \leq t_G \leq t_1 + 26) \rightarrow (t_G \leq t_1 + 30)$, by Theorem 15 we have the following inequality for term (52).

$P_{now}(\exists t_G, t_G' \, (t_G \leq t_1 + 30) \wedge OCCURS(\text{get(table)}, t_G, t_G') \,| \qquad (54)$
$\quad OCC(\text{drive(home,restaurant)}, t_1 + 1, t_1 + 11) \wedge$
$\quad OCC(\text{start(car)}, t_1, t_1 + 1)) \geq$

$P_{now}(\exists t_G, t_G' \, (t_1 + 11 \leq t_G \leq t_1 + 26) \wedge OCCURS(\text{get(table)}, t_G, t_G') \,|$
$\quad OCC(\text{drive(home,restaurant)}, t_1 + 1, t_1 + 11) \wedge$
$\quad OCC(\text{start(car)}, t_1, t_1 + 1))$

By assumption (34) and Axiom FOL5, we have

$P_{now}(\exists t_G, t_G' \, (t_1 + 11 \leq t_G \leq t_1 + 26) \wedge OCCURS(\text{get(table)}, t_G, t_G') \,| \qquad (55)$
$\quad OCC(\text{drive(home,restaurant)}, t_1 + 1, t_1 + 11) \wedge$
$\quad OCC(\text{start(car)}, t_1, t_1 + 1)) \geq$

$P_{now}(\exists t_G, t_G' \, (t_1 + 11 \leq t_G \leq t_1 + 26) \wedge OCCURS(\text{get(table)}, t_G, t_G') \,|$
$\quad OCC(\text{drive(home,restaurant)}, t_1 + 1, t_1 + 11))$

By the definition of c-prob, term (53) may be written as

$P_{now}(OCC(\text{drive(home,restaurant)}, t_1 + 1, t_1 + 11) \,| \qquad (56)$
$\quad ATT(\text{drive(home,restaurant)}, t_1 + 1) \wedge OCC(\text{start(car)}, t_1, t_1 + 1)) \cdot$

$P_{now}(OCC(\text{start(car)}, t_1, t_1 + 1) \,| \qquad (57)$
$\quad ATT(\text{start(car)}, t_1) \wedge ATT(\text{drive(home,restaurant)}, t_1 + 1))$

By assumption (35) and Axiom FOL5, we have the following inequality for term (57).

$P_{now}(OCC(\text{start(car)}, t_1, t_1 + 1) \,| \qquad (58)$
$\quad ATT(\text{start(car)}, t_1) \wedge ATT(\text{drive(home,restaurant)}, t_1 + 1)) \geq$

$P_{now}(OCC(\text{start(car)}, t_1, t_1 + 1) \,| ATT(\text{start(car)}, t_1))$

So we have the following inequality for term (42).

$$P_{now}(\exists t_G, t_G' \, (t_G \leq t_1 + 30) \wedge OCCURS(\text{get(table)}, t_G, t_G') \wedge$$
$$OCC(\text{drive(home,restaurant)}, t_1 + 1, t_1 + 11) \wedge$$
$$OCC(\text{start(car)}, t_1, t_1 + 1) \, |$$
$$ATT(\text{drive(home,restaurant)}, t_1 + 1) \wedge ATT(\text{start(car)}, t_1)) \geq$$
$$P_{now}(\exists t_G, t_G' \, (t_1 + 11 \leq t_G \leq t_1 + 26) \wedge OCCURS(\text{get(table)}, t_G, t_G') \, | \qquad (59)$$
$$OCC(\text{drive(home,restaurant)}, t_1 + 1, t_1 + 11)) \cdot$$
$$P_{now}(OCC(\text{drive(home,restaurant)}, t_1 + 1, t_1 + 11) \, | \qquad\qquad (60)$$
$$ATT(\text{drive(home,restaurant)}, t_1 + 1) \wedge OCC(\text{start(car)}, t_1, t_1 + 1) \cdot$$
$$P_{now}(OCC(\text{start(car)}, t_1, t_1 + 1) \, | \, ATT(\text{start(car)}, t_1)) \qquad\qquad (61)$$

Now we derive numerical bounds for the terms (59), (60), (61). First we derive a bound for term (59). By Axiom FOL5 and (30),

$$P_{now}(\exists t, t' \, (t_1 + 11 \leq t \leq t_1 + 26) \wedge OCCURS(\text{get(table)}, t, t') \, | \qquad (62)$$
$$OCC(\text{drive(home,restaurant)}, t_1 + 1, t_1 + 11) \wedge$$
$$\neg \exists t_p, t_p' \, (t_p' < t_1 + 11 \leq t_p' + 60) \wedge OCCURS(\text{performance}, t_p, t_p')) \geq .8$$

By Theorem 15 and (41),

$$P_{now}(\neg \exists t, t' \, (t' < t_1 + 11 \leq t' + 60) \wedge OCCURS(\text{performance}, t, t')) = 1 \qquad (63)$$

So by the assumption that ramification conditions are independent of the action occurrence, the definition of c-prob, and (62) and (63),

$$P_{now}(\exists t, t' \, (t_1 + 11 \leq t \leq t_1 + 26) \wedge OCCURS(\text{get(table)}, t, t') \, | \qquad (64)$$
$$OCC(\text{drive(home,restaurant)}, t_1 + 1, t_1 + 11)) \geq .8$$

Next we derive a value for term (60). By Axiom FOL5 and (31),

$$P_{now}(OCC(\text{drive(home,restaurant)}, t_1 + 1, t_1 + 11) \, | \qquad\qquad (65)$$
$$ATT(\text{drive(home,restaurant)}, t_1 + 1) \wedge$$
$$OCC(\text{start(car)}, t_1, t_1 + 1)) = 1$$

Finally we derive a bound for term (61). By Axiom FOL5 and (28),

$$P_{now}(OCC(\text{start(car)}, t_1, t_1 + 1) \, | \qquad\qquad (66)$$
$$ATT(\text{start(car)}, t_1) \wedge HOLDS((\text{temp} > 32), t_1, t_1 + 1)) \geq .95$$

By Theorem 23 and (37),

$$P_{now}(HOLDS((\text{temp} > 32), t_1, t_1 + 1)) \geq .8 \qquad\qquad (67)$$

So by the assumption that executability conditions are independent of the action attempt, the definition of c-prob, and (66) and (67),

$$P_{now}(OCC(\text{start(car)}, t_1, t_1 + 1) \, | \qquad\qquad (68)$$
$$ATT(\text{start(car)}, t_1)) \geq (.8)(.95) = .76$$

From (63), (64), and (68) we obtain a lower bound on the probability of term (42) of

$$(.8)(1)(.76) = .60 \qquad (69)$$

Finally, combining the probability values from (47), (51), and (69) we obtain the lower bound on the chance that the plan achieves the goal:

$$P_{now}(\exists t_G, t'_G \, (t_G \leq t_1 + 30) \land OCCURS(get(table), t_G, t'_G) \land \qquad (70)$$
$$OCC(drive(home, restaurant), t_1 + 1, t_1 + 11) \land$$
$$OCC(start(car), t_1, t_1 + 1) \mid$$
$$ATT(drive(home, restaurant), t_1 + 1) \land ATT(start(car), t_1)) \cdot$$
$$P_{now}(FEAS(drive(home, restaurant), t_1 + 1) \mid ATT(start(car), t_1)) \cdot$$
$$P_{now}(FEAS(start(car), t_1)) \geq (.60)(.95)(.95) = .54$$

8.1   A Note on Represeting Temporally Quantified Conditions

Suppose we want to represent the fact that the chance of ψ given that ϕ holds or occurs at some time (it doesn't matter when) is α. This can be represented by either of the two sentences:

$$\forall t \, P_{now}(\psi \mid \phi(t)) = \alpha \qquad (71)$$

$$P_{now}(\psi \mid \exists t \, \phi(t)) = \alpha, \qquad (72)$$

where $\phi(t)$ is some temporal formula. For example, we could represent the fact that dropping a vase has a high chance of breaking it with one of the two sentences:

$$\forall t_b, t \, P_{now}(\exists t'_b \, HOLDS(broken, t_b, t'_b) \mid OCC(dropped, t, t_b)) = .9 \qquad (73)$$

$$\forall t_b \, P_{now}(\exists t'_b \, HOLDS(broken, t_b, t'_b) \mid \exists t \, OCC(dropped, t, t_b)) = .9 \qquad (74)$$

If we know that the chance the vase is dropped during the interval t_1 to t_2 is .7,

$$P_{now}(OCC(dropped, t_1, t_2)) = .7, \qquad (75)$$

we can use either sentence (73) or (74) to derive the lower bound of .63 on the chance that the vase is broken. To get a precise value for the chance that the vase is broken using sentence (73), we would additionally need to know

$$\forall t_b, t \, P_{now}(\exists t'_b \, HOLDS(broken, t_b, t'_b) \mid \neg OCC(dropped, t, t_b)) = \alpha \qquad (76)$$

for some α. Using sentence (74), we cannot obtain a precise value for the chance of the vase being broken based on our knowledge of the chance of the specific instance (75) since the specific instance $OCC(dropped, t_1, t_2)$ only entails the existentially quantified formula
$\exists t \, OCC(dropped, t, t_2)$. So the best we can do with the existentially quantified representation is to derive a lower bound.

Now suppose we wish to know the probability that the vase is broken given a specific instance of the drop action. This can be obtained from (73) by universal instantiation. It cannot be obtained from (74) because there is in general no relation between the probabiltiy of a formula ψ given a formula ϕ and the probability of ψ given a formula γ that that entails ϕ. So it would appear that the universally quantified form (71) is more useful than the existentially quantified form (72) for the types of inferences we are interested in performing.

9 Construction Planning System

9.1 The Problem

In this chapter we present a simple planning algorithm in order to demonstrate the methodology presented earlier. Following that methodology, a specialized planning algorithm is presented. The meanings of the data structures and assumptions in the algorithm are specified in terms of sentences of $\mathcal{L}_{tca}$. The algorithm itself is characterized in terms of inference over these sentences. Using the specification in terms of $\mathcal{L}_{tca}$, we then prove part of the algorithm correct. The planning algorithm presented has been implemented in Common Lisp. In the last section of this chapter, we demonstrate the algorithm by giving the planner the simple task of planning the construction of a warehouse.

The application domain is building construction planning. The task is to choose a building design that will allow the building to be constructed as quickly as possible. For each functional component of the building to be constructed, several physical options may be available. For example, the frame may be steel, precast concrete, or cast-in-place concrete. The different options for a component may differ in terms of the time and resources required for their installation. For example, installation of a steel frame can be performed more quickly than installation of a cast-in-place concrete frame but the steel frame requires both a crane and a steel crew, while the cast-in-place concrete frame requires neither. Our goal is to complete construction of the building in the minimum amount of time. So the planning problem requires selecting the combination of building components that results in the earliest completion of the construction project. The planning problem can be divided into two distinct tasks: selection of the combination of construction components and scheduling of the activities[16] associated with the installation of the components.

The scheduling task is the problem of finding the construction schedule that results in the earliest completion of the construction project for a given combination of construction components. Two types of constraints are present in the scheduling task: precedence constraints and resource contention. Precedence constraints arise because, for various reasons, the installation of one component cannot occur before the installation of another. For example, the roof cannot be installed before the frame because the frame supports the roof. And the walls cannot be installed before the plumbing because the walls cover the plumbing. Resource contention occurs when two or more activities require the same limited resource. If insufficient resources are available, not all the activities that require that resource can be performed concurrently. If the activities cannot all be performed concurrently, several possible orderings may be possible. For example, installing roof trusses and wall panels both require the use of a crane. If only one crane is present, the two activities cannot be performed concurrently, so one must precede the other. We wish to find the schedule, i.e., the ordering of activities, that minimizes the completion time. But we may not know precisely how

---

[16] In keeping with the terminology of the domain, actions will be called activities.

much of each resource will be available at construction time. So we have probabilities associated with the quantities of resources that will be available. Thus the scheduling task becomes one of finding the earliest *expected* completion time for a given combination of construction components. The planning task then simply becomes the selection of that component combination with the earliest expected completion time.

We will simplify the problem by making a number of assumptions. We assume that once an installation activity is completed, the component remains installed. This means that the building is completed once all the installation activities have occurred. Since we are only interested in the effects of activities as they relate to completion of the building (e.g. we are not interested in costs), this assumption allows us to ignore effects. By also assuming that all activities are certainly feasible, we limit the problem to reasoning about the executability of activities.

In keeping with the two types of constraints, the scheduling algorithm can be divided into two distinct parts. The first part concerns the scheduling of activities based only on precedence constraints. This scheduling algorithm is known in the literature on project and process scheduling as the Critical Path Method (CPM)[6, 79]. The other part of the algorithm generates possible precedence constraints among the activities that contend for each given resource. The overall scheduling algorithm works by generating all possible sets of precedence relations among activities that contend for each resource. Each possible set of precedence relations is combined with the initially specified precedence relations and the CPM algorithm is used to determine the earliest possible completion time for the resulting activity network. The various completion times are then weighted by the probabilities of the resource combinations to determine the earliest expected completion time for the given set of activities.

We first present the data structures and algorithm for the CPM portion of the scheduling task and then add the facility to reason about contention for probabilistic resources.

9.2 The CPM Algorithm

Data Structures. The basic data structure for the CPM algorithm is the *activity network*. The nodes in the activity network represent the activities to be scheduled and directed links represent the precedence relations among activities. Each node is labeled with the activity name, its duration, and its earliest possible start time. A link from activity A_1 to activity A_2 means that A_1 must precede A_2. Each element of the network data structure has a precise meaning in terms of the logic $\mathcal{L}_{tca}$.

A node for an activity A_1 with duration d_{A_1} that has no incoming links represents the fact that A_1 can be performed at any time:

$$\forall t_{A_1} \, P_{now}(OCC(A_1, t_{A_1}, t_{A_1} + d_{A_1}) \mid ATT(A_1, t_{A_1})) = 1$$

A node for an activity B that has an incoming link from each of a set of nodes $A_1, ..., A_n$ as shown in Fig. 23 represents the fact that B cannot be performed if

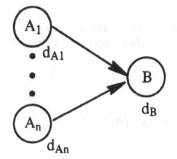

Fig. 23. Node with multiple incoming links.

not preceded by the occurrence of each of the A_i. So we have one sentence for each of the A_i, of the form

$$\forall t_B, t'_B \, P_{now}(OCC(B, t_B, t'_B) \mid \neg \exists t_{A_i}, t'_{A_i} \, (t'_{A_i} \leq t_B) \wedge OCC(A_i, t_{A_i}, t'_{A_i})) = 0$$

The node for B also represents the fact that B can be performed if preceded by each of the A_i:

$$\forall t_{A_1}, t'_{A_1}, ..., t_{A_n}, t'_{A_n}, t_B \, (t'_{A_1} \leq t_B) \wedge ... \wedge (t'_{A_n} \leq t_B) \rightarrow$$
$$P_{now}(OCC(B, t_B, t_B + d_B) \mid ATT(B, t_B) \wedge_i OCC(A_i, t_{A_i}, t'_{A_i})) = 1$$

Notice that the conjunction of the occurrences of the A_i plays the role of an executability condition in this sentence.

Assumptions. One of the main benefits of proving the correctness of the algorithm is that it forces us to make explicit and precise the assumptions in the algorithm. We assume that the activities are unique, i.e. they are attempted only once:

$$P_{now}(\forall t, t' \, ATT(A, t) \wedge ATT(A, t') \rightarrow (t = t')) = 1 \tag{77}$$

and they occur only once:

$$P_{now}(\forall t, t', t'', t''' \, OCC(A, t, t') \wedge OCC(A, t'', t''') \rightarrow \tag{78}$$
$$(t = t'') \wedge (t' = t''')) = 1$$

Algorithm. Assume the activity network has no cycles, so we have a directed acyclic graph. Add as start node *Start* with duration zero and outgoing links to all nodes that do not already have incoming links. Add an end node *End* with duration zero and incoming links from all nodes that do not already have outgoing links. For a network of activities A_i, the goal of the algorithm is to find the earliest times t_{A_i} such that

$$P_{now}(\wedge_i OCC(A_i, t_{A_i}, t'_{A_i}) \mid \wedge_i ATT(A_i, t_{A_i})) = 1$$

The CPM algorithm works by propagating early start times for activities forward through the network as follows.

Algorithm 1 *CPM Algorithm*

For each node N let $succ(N)$ be the set of nodes to which N has a link and let $dur(N)$ be the duration of N. Initialize the early start time (EST) of all nodes in the network to zero.
FRONTIER = {Start}
Repeat

- *For each N_i in FRONTIER, for each node N_j in $succ(N_i)$,*
  $EST(N_j) = max(EST(N_j), EST(N_i)+dur(N_i))$.
- *FRONTIER = $\bigcup_{N_i \in FRONTIER} succ(N_i)$*

Until FRONTIER = ∅
The earliest possible completion time for the network of activities is then EST(End).

Proof of Correctness. We now prove the correctness of the CPM algorithm using the proof theory of $\mathcal{L}_{tca}$. We prove soundness by showing that the EST computed for each node by the CPM algorithm is entailed by the sentences represented by the activity network. We prove completeness by showing that the computed EST is less than or equal to every start time entailed by the sentences.

Soundness. Suppose we have an activity network N with activities A_i and B. Suppose that B has duration d_B and links from two nodes A_m and A_n, with durations d_m and d_n, respectively.[17] Suppose we know that for some times t_i and t_i'

$$P_{now}(\wedge_i OCC(A_i, t_i, t_i') \mid \wedge_i ATT(A_i, t_i)) = 1 \tag{79}$$

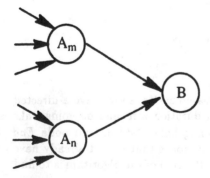

Fig. 24. Activity network.

---

[17] We only prove the case for two links. The proof of soundness follows by straightforwardly generalizing the number of incoming links.

The resulting network N' is shown in Fig. 24. The links from A_m and A_n represent, among others, the sentence

$$\forall t_{A_m}, t'_{A_m}, t_{A_n}, t'_{A_n}, t_B\ (t'_{A_m} \leq t_B) \wedge (t'_{A_n} \leq t_B) \rightarrow \tag{80}$$
$$P_{now}(OCC(B, t_B, t_B + d_B)\,|\,ATT(B, t_B) \wedge OCC(A_m, t_{A_m}, t'_{A_m}) \wedge$$
$$OCC(A_n, t_{A_n}, t'_{A_n}) = 1$$

Instantiate the start times t_{A_m} and t_{A_n} in (80) to t_m and t_n, respectively and instantiate the end times t'_{A_m} and t'_{A_n} to t'_m and t'_n, respectively. Given these start and end times, the CPM algorithm will infer that

$$P_{now}(OCC(B, max(t'_m, t'_n), max(t'_m, t'_n) + d_B) \wedge_i OCC(A_i, t_i, t'_i)\,| \tag{81}$$
$$ATT(B, max(t'_m, t'_n)) \wedge_i ATT(A_i, t_i)) = 1$$

So we want to show that this follows from (80). To show this, we instantiate the start time of B to $t_B = max(t'_m, t'_n)$. Then since

$$t'_m \leq max(t'_m, t'_n)$$

and

$$t'_n \leq max(t'_m, t'_n)$$

we have from (80) that

$$P_{now}(OCC(B, max(t'_m, t'_n), max(t'_m, t'_n) + d_B)\,| \tag{82}$$
$$ATT(B, max(t'_m, t'_n)) \wedge OCC(A_m, t_m, t'_m) \wedge OCC(A_n, t_n, t'_n)) = 1$$

By the definition of c-prob, the left-hand side of (81) may be written as

$$P_{now}(OCC(B, max(t'_m, t'_n), max(t'_m, t'_n) + d_B)\,| \tag{83}$$
$$ATT(B, max(t'_m, t'_n)) \wedge_i ATT(A_i, t_i) \wedge_i OCC(A_i, t_i, t'_i)) \cdot$$
$$P_{now}(\wedge_i OCC(A_i, t_i, t'_i)\,|\,ATT(B, max(t'_m, t'_n)) \wedge_i ATT(A_i, t_i)) \tag{84}$$

It follows from (82) by Theorem 16 that term (83) has probability 1:

$$P_{now}(OCC(B, max(t'_m, t'_n), max(t'_m, t'_n) + d_B)\,|$$
$$ATT(B, max(t'_m, t'_n)) \wedge_i ATT(A_i, t_i) \wedge_i OCC(A_i, t_i, t'_i)) = 1$$

and again by Theorem 16 it follows from (79) that term (84) has probability 1:

$$P_{now}(\wedge_i OCC(A_i, t_i, t'_i)\,|\,ATT(B, max(t'_m, t'_n)) \wedge_i ATT(A_i, t_i)) = 1$$

So we have the desired result:

$$P_{now}(OCC(B, max(t'_m, t'_n), max(t'_m, t'_n) + d_B) \wedge_i OCC(A_i, t_i, t'_i)\,|$$
$$ATT(B, max(t'_m, t'_n)) \wedge_i ATT(A_i, t_i)) = 1$$

Completeness. We wish to show that the CPM algorithm is complete, i.e. that it derives the earliest start times for all nodes in an activity network. We prove completeness by induction on the depth of the activity network. The CPM algorithm is trivially complete for a network of depth one, i.e. no arcs. Suppose we have a network N of depth n with nodes A_i. Suppose the CPM algorithm is complete for N so that it computes the EST's for the t_i for the activities A_i. We create a new network N' from N by adding a node B with duration d_B and links to B from two nodes A_m and A_n, with durations d_m and d_n, respectively.

Suppose without loss of generality that $t'_n \leq t'_m$. We want to show that B cannot occur earlier than $max(t'_m, t'_n)$:

$$\forall t_B \ (t_B < t'_m) \ \rightarrow \ P_{now}(OCC(B, t_B, t_B + d_B)) = 0$$

Suppose that

$$(t_B < t'_m) \tag{85}$$

By assumption (78) we have

$$\forall t, t' \ OCC(A_m, t_m, t'_m) \wedge OCC(A_m, t, t') \ \rightarrow \ (t = t_m) \vee (t' = t'_m)$$

From which we have the following derivation

$$OCC(A_m, t_m, t'_m) \ \rightarrow \ \neg \exists t, t' \ OCC(A_m, t, t') \wedge [(t \neq t_m) \vee (t' \neq t'_m)]$$

$$OCC(A_m, t_m, t'_m) \ \rightarrow \ \neg \exists t, t' \ OCC(A_m, t, t') \wedge (t' \neq t'_m)$$

$$OCC(A_m, t_m, t'_m) \ \rightarrow \ \neg \exists t, t' \ OCC(A_m, t, t') \wedge (t' < t'_m)$$

And so by (85)

$$OCC(A_m, t_m, t'_m) \ \rightarrow \ \neg \exists t, t' \ OCC(A_m, t, t') \wedge (t' \leq t_B) \tag{86}$$

The link to B from A_m represents, among others, the sentence

$$\forall t_B, t'_B \ P_{now}(OCC(B, t_B, t'_B) \ | \tag{87}$$
$$\neg \exists t_{A_m}, t'_{A_m} \ (t'_{A_m} \leq t_B) \wedge OCC(A_m, t_m, t'_m)) = 0$$

Hence by (85), (86), and (87), we have the desired result:

$$\forall t_B \ (t_B < t'_m) \ \rightarrow \ P_{now}(OCC(B, t_B, t_B + d_B)) = 0$$

9.3   Incorporating Resource Dependence

Data Structures. In reasoning about concurrent activities, we will find it useful to define a shorthand notation that specifies whether k intervals overlap:

$$overlap(t_1, t'_1, ..., t_k, t'_k) \ \equiv \ \exists t \ \wedge_{i=1}^{k} (t_i < t < t'_i)$$

In order to reason about resource dependence we extend the activity network representation. Activities are represented by *activity nodes* and precedence

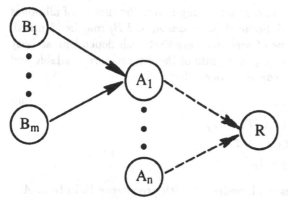

Fig. 25. Extended activity network.

relations by *precedence links*. Resources are represented by *resource nodes* and the dependence of an activity on a resource is represented by a *dependence link* from the activity to the resource. Such an extended activity network is shown in Fig. 25. The dashed lines represent resource dependence links and the solid lines represent precedence links. So in this net, activities A_1 through A_n require resource R and activities B_1 through B_m must precede activity A_1. We assume that each activity requires at most one unit of each resource. If there are fewer resource units available than activities whose occurrence depends on that resource, not all the activities can be executed concurrently. A resource node R with dependence links from n activities $A_1, ..., A_n$ represents three types of sentences. The first type says that for each k between 1 and the $n - 1$ if only k units of the resource are available then $k + 1$ activities cannot occur concurrently:

$$\forall t_{A_i}, t'_{A_i} \, overlap(t_{A_i}, t'_{A_i}) \; \rightarrow \tag{88}$$
$$P_{now}(\wedge_i OCC(A_i, t_{A_i}, t'_{A_i}) \mid HOLDS(num(R, k), \max(t_{A_i}), \min(t'_{A_i})))) = 0,$$

where i ranges over $k + 1$ of the n indices, and k is an integer between 1 and $n - 1$.

The second type of sentence needs to take into account both the resource dependence and precedence links. It says that if k units of the resource are available and k of the dependent activities are not occurring over intervals that overlap with some dependent activity A, and all the activities that must precede A do occur before it, then A can certainly be executed. For each k between 1 and $n - 1$ we have one such sentence for each activity A dependent on R:

$$\forall t_A, t_{B_j}, t'_{B_j} \; \wedge_j (t'_{B_j} \leq t_A) \; \rightarrow \tag{89}$$
$$P_{now}(OCC(A, t_A, t_A + d_A) \mid ATT(A, t_A) \wedge$$
$$\qquad HOLDS(num(R, k), t_A, t_A + d_A) \wedge$$
$$\qquad \neg[\exists t_{A_i}, t'_{A_i} \; \wedge_i \, overlap(t_{A_i}, t'_{A_i}, t_A, t_A + d_A) \wedge_i OCC(A_i, t_{A_i}, t'_{A_i})]$$
$$\qquad \wedge_j OCC(B_j, t_{B_j}, t'_{B_j})) = 1,$$

where i ranges over k of the n indices and j ranges over the indices of all nodes B_j with precedence links from A. Some of the nodes A_i and B_j may be identical.

For each $k \geq n$, the third type of sentence says that each dependent activity A can certainly be executed as long as k units of the resource are available and all the activities that must precede A do occur before it.

$$\forall t_A, t_{B_j}, t'_{B_j} \; \wedge_j (t'_{B_j} \leq t_A) \to \tag{90}$$
$$P_{now}(OCC(A, t_A, t_A + d_A) \mid ATT(A, t_A) \wedge$$
$$HOLDS(\text{num}(R, k), t_A, t_A + d_A)$$
$$\wedge_j OCC(B_j, t_{B_j}, t'_{B_j})) = 1,$$

where j ranges over the indices of all nodes B_j with precedence links from A.

Activity nodes with no resource dependence links represent the same sentences as in the simple activity networks.

Assumptions. We assume that the available number of each resource is independent of the activities. So for each resource R we have a set of sentences of the form:

$$\forall k, t, t', t'' \; P_{now}(HOLDS(\text{num}(R, k), t', t'') \mid \wedge_i ATT(A_i, t_{A_i}) \tag{91}$$
$$\wedge_j OCC(A_j, t_{A_j}, t'_{A_j})) =$$
$$P_{now}(HOLDS(\text{num}(R, k), t', t'')),$$

where $\wedge_i ATT(A_i, t_{A_i})$ and $\wedge_j OCC(A_j, t_{A_j}, t'_{A_j})$ represent any conjunctions of activity attempts and occurrences.

The Planning Algorithm.

Algorithm 2 *Planning Algorithm*
Let pca's be the set of possible combinations of activities, based on the available construction options.
Let pcrq's be the set of possible combinations of resource quantities.
Let Prob(pcrq) be the chance of pcrq $\in$ pcrq's.
Let EECT(pca) be the earliest expected completion time of pca $\in$ pca's.
Let ECT(pca,pcrq) be the earliest completion time of the best plan composed of the activities in pca, with respect to the combination of resource quantities pcrq. ECT is calculated by running the CPM algorithm on each ordering of the activities consistent with the resource requirements of the activities and the resource quantities specified by pcrq. The precise algorithm is given below.

> *For each pca $\in$ pca's*
> *For each pcrq $\in$ pcrq's*
> *EECT(pca) = ECT(pca,pcrq) * Prob(pcrq)*

Choose the combination of activities with the lowest EECT.

Algorithm 3 *Computation of ECT(activities, resources)*
Let dependents(res) be the set of activities that use resource res.
Let quant(res) be the available quantity of resource res.
Let poss-ords(res) be the concurrency maximizing possible orderings of dependents(res), allowed by quant(res). For example, if we have two units of a resource R with three dependent activities A, B, C, there are six possible concurrency maximizing orderings: $(\{AB\}C), (C\{AB\}), (\{AC\}B)$, etc. The set notation means that the activities are performed concurrently.
Let poss-ord-combos be the set of all combinations of possible activity orderings, taking one ordering from each of poss-ords(res_i) for all $res_i \in$ resources.
Let core-net be the activity network for activities, based only on their precedence constraints.

> For each $poc_i \in$ poss-ord-combos
> Create a new net (net_i) by adding the links for poc to core-net.
> Compute the $EST(End_i)$ for net_i with the CPM algorithm.
> $ECT(activities, resources) = \min_i EST(End_i)$

Example Derivation. Due to the complexity of the problem, proving the correctness of the planning algorithm is beyond the scope of this monograph. We can however illustrate the derivations performed by the algorithm on a simple resource dependence example. Suppose we have two activities A_1 and A_2 that both use one unit of resource R. Suppose we either have one or two units of resource R available:

$$\forall t, t' \; HOLDS(\text{num}(R, 1), t, t') \leftrightarrow \neg HOLDS(\text{num}(R, 2), t, t') \tag{92}$$

$$\forall t, t', n \; HOLDS(\text{num}(R, n), t, t') \rightarrow n = 1 \vee n = 2 \tag{93}$$

We assume that the number of resources is independent of attempting both activities:

$$\forall t, t', t'', n \; P_{now}(HOLDS(\text{num}(R, n), t', t'') \mid \tag{94}$$
$$ATT(A_1, t) \wedge ATT(A_2, t)) =$$
$$P_{now}(HOLDS(\text{num}(R, n), t', t''))$$

The influence of resource availability on the executability of the activities can be represented as follows. If only one unit of the resource is available, the activities cannot be executed concurrently:

$$\forall t_{A_1}, t'_{A_1}, t_{A_2}, t'_{A_2} \; \text{overlap}(t_{A_1}, t'_{A_1}, t_{A_2}, t'_{A_2}) \rightarrow \tag{95}$$
$$P_{now}(OCC(A_1, t_{A_1}, t'_{A_1}) \wedge OCC(A_2, t_{A_2}, t'_{A_2}) \mid$$
$$HOLDS(\text{num}(R, 1), \max(t_{A_1}, t_{A_2}), \min(t'_{A_1}, t'_{A_2})) = 0$$

If two units of the resource are available, each activity can be executed at any time, which means that the two may be executed concurrently.

$$\forall t_{A_1} \; P_{now}(OCC(A_1, t_{A_1}, t_{A_1} + d_{A_1}) \mid \tag{96}$$
$$ATT(A_1, t_{A_1}) \wedge HOLDS(\text{num}(R, 2), t_{A_1}, t_{A_1} + d_{A_1})) = 1$$

$$\forall t_{A_1}\, P_{now}(OCC(A_2, t_{A_2}, t_{A_2} + d_{A_2})\,| \tag{97}$$
$$ATT(A_2, t_{A_2}) \land HOLDS(\text{num}(R, 2), t_{A_2}, t_{A_2} + d_{A_2})) = 1$$

The activities can be executed sequentially if at least a single unit of the resource is available, i.e., each activity can be executed as long as the other activity is not already in the process of occurring:

$$\forall t_{A_1}\, P_{now}(OCC(A_1, t_{A_1}, t_{A_1} + d_{A_1})\,| \tag{98}$$
$$ATT(A_1, t_{A_1}) \land$$
$$\neg[\exists t_{A_2}, t'_{A_2}(t_{A_2} \leq t_{A_1} < t'_{A_2}) \land OCC(A_2, t_{A_2}, t'_{A_2})]) = 1$$

$$\forall t_{A_1}\, P_{now}(OCC(A_2, t_{A_2}, t_{A_2} + d_{A_2})\,| \tag{99}$$
$$ATT(A_2, t_{A_2}) \land$$
$$\neg[\exists t_{A_1}, t'_{A_1}(t_{A_1} \leq t_{A_2} < t'_{A_1}) \land OCC(A_1, t_{A_1}, t'_{A_1})]) = 1$$

Now suppose that the chance we will have one unit of resource available is α and the chance the will have two is $1 - \alpha$:

$$P_{now}(HOLDS(\text{num}(R, 1), t_0, t_0 + d_{A_1} + d_{A_2})) = \alpha \tag{100}$$

$$P_{now}(HOLDS(\text{num}(R, 2), t_0, t_0 + d_{A_1} + d_{A_2})) = 1 - \alpha \tag{101}$$

What is the chance that the two activities can be executed concurrently? We first derive the chance if two units of the resource are available. It follows from (96) and (97) by Theorems 16 and 17 that the two activities may be executed concurrently, given two units of the resource:

$$\forall t\, P_{now}(OCC(A_1, t, t + d_{A_1}) \land OCC(A_2, t, t + d_{A_2})\,| \tag{102}$$
$$ATT(A_1, t) \land ATT(A_2, t) \land$$
$$HOLDS(\text{num}(R, 2), t, \max(t + d_{A_1}, t + d_{A_2}))) = 1$$

By the definition of c-prob it follows from assumption (94), (101) and (102) that

$$P_{now}(OCC(A_1, t_0, t_0 + d_{A_1}) \land OCC(A_2, t_0, t_0 + d_{A_2}) \land \tag{103}$$
$$HOLDS(\text{num}(R, 2), t_0, t_0 + d_{A_1} + d_{A_2})\,|$$
$$ATT(A_1, t_0) \land ATT(A_2, t_0)) = 1 - \alpha$$

Now we derive the chance the two activities can be executed concurrently if only one unit of the resource is available. First, since durations are positive, we have

$$\forall t\, (t \leq t < t + d_{A_2})$$

So we have

$$\forall t\, overlap(t, t + d_{A_1}, t, t + d_{A_2})$$

Hence it follows from (95) that

$$\forall t\, P_{now}(OCC(A_1, t, t + d_{A_1}) \land OCC(A_2, t, t + d_{A_2})\,| \tag{104}$$
$$HOLDS(\text{num}(R, 1), t, \min(t + d_{A_1}, t + d_{A_2}))) = 0$$

By the definition of c-prob, it follows from (104) that the chance they can be executed concurrently with only one unit of resource available is zero:

$$\forall t \, P_{now}(OCC(A_1, t, t+d_{A_1}) \wedge OCC(A_2, t, t+d_{A_2}) \wedge \tag{105}$$
$$HOLDS(\text{num}(R, 1), t, \min(t+d_{A_1}, t+d_{A_2})) \mid$$
$$ATT(A_1, t) \wedge ATT(A_2, t)) = 0$$

By Axiom P2 and the definition of c-prob, we can finally infer from (103) and (105) that there is a $(1-\alpha)\%$ chance the two activities can be executed concurrently:

$$P_{now}(OCC(A_1, t_0, t_0+d_{A_1}) \wedge OCC(A_2, t_0, t_0+d_{A_2}) \mid \tag{106}$$
$$ATT(A_1, t_0) \wedge ATT(A_2, t_0)) = 1 - \alpha$$

Next we derive the chance that the two activities can be executed sequentially. This, of course, will turn out to be one. First, from (99) and (78) it follows by Theorem 16 that

$$P_{now}(OCC(A_2, t_{A_1}+d_{A_1}, t_{A_1}+d_{A_1}+d_{A_2}) \mid \tag{107}$$
$$ATT(A_2, t_{A_1}+d_{A_1}) \wedge OCC(A_1, t_{A_1}, t_{A_1}+d_{A_1})) = 1$$

By Axiom ACT1 it follows from (107) that

$$P_{now}(OCC(A_2, t_{A_1}+d_{A_1}, t_{A_1}+d_{A_1}+d_{A_2}) \mid \tag{108}$$
$$ATT(A_1, t_{A_1}) \wedge ATT(A_2, t_{A_1}+d_{A_1}) \wedge OCC(A_1, t_{A_1}, t_{A_1}+d_{A_1})) = 1$$

It follows from (77) by Axiom ACT1 that

$$\forall t, t', t'' \, ATT(A_2, t) \wedge OCC(A_2, t', t'') \rightarrow (t = t') \tag{109}$$

So from (98) and (109) we have by Theorem 16 that

$$P_{now}(OCC(A_1, t_{A_1}, t_{A_1}+d_{A_1}) \mid \tag{110}$$
$$ATT(A_1, t_{A_1}) \wedge ATT(A_2, t_{A_1}+d_{A_1})) = 1$$

Finally, by the definition of c-prob, it follows from (108) and (110) that

$$P_{now}(OCC(A_1, t, t+d_{A_1}) \wedge OCC(A_2, t+d_{A_1}, t+d_{A_1}+d_{A_2}) \mid \tag{111}$$
$$ATT(A_1, t) \wedge ATT(A_2, t+d_{A_1})) = 1$$

Assume that we will execute the activities concurrently if possible. If the start time for the activities is t_0 in both concurrent and sequential execution then the expected completion time for both activities is

$$(1-\alpha)(\max(t_0+d_{A_1}, t_0+d_{A_2}) + (\alpha)(t_0+d_{A_1}+d_{A_2})$$

9.4 Construction Planning Example

We demonstrate the planning algorithm with the simple example of planning the construction of a warehouse. The warehouse will consist of five functional components: foundation, frame, wall panels, roof trusses, roof panels. For the frame we may choose among three options: steel, precast concrete, and cast-in-place concrete. For the roof panels we have two options: small roof panels and large roof panels. These options differ in the durations and resource requirements of their associated installation activities. The installation activities for the various components are described in the table below.

component	duration	resources	preceded by
foundation	4	–	–
steel frame	8	crane, steel crew	foundation
precast frame	9	crane	foundation
cast-in-place frame	10	–	foundation
assemble roof trusses	6	steel crew	–
install roof trusses	2	crane, steel crew	assemble roof trusses
wall panels	4	crane	frame
large roof panels	4	crane	install roof trusses
small roof panels	7	–	install roof trusses

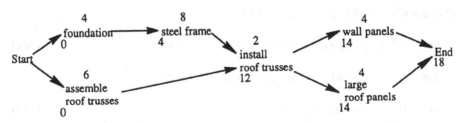

Fig. 26. Best plan for two cranes and two steel crews.

Suppose we are certain to have two cranes and two steel crews available. The planner selects to use a steel frame and the large roof panels. Since we are certain of the resources available, we have a single best plan, shown in Fig. 26. The EST's are shown at the lower left corner of each nodes and the durations are shown above each node.

Now suppose that we are certain to have only one crane and one steel crew available. The best plan for the above selection of construction options (i.e. using a steel frame and large roof panels) is shown in Fig. 27. Notice that installation of the steel frame must now occur after the assembly of the roof trusses since

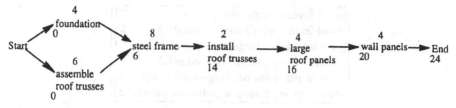

Fig. 27. Sub-optimal plan for one crane and one steel crew.

only one steel crew is available. Also the availability of only one crane constrains the wall panels to be installed after the roof panels.

Considering other construction options, the best plan is to use a precast concrete frame and small roof panels, as shown in Fig. 28. These choices maximize concurrency since installation of the precast concrete frame does not require a steel crew and installation the small roof panels does not require a crane.

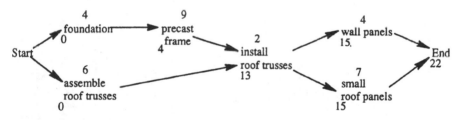

Fig. 28. Best plan for one crane and one steel crew.

Finally suppose there is an equal chance we will have one or two cranes available and an equal chance we will have one or two steel crews available. We assume that the chances of the two resource quantities are independent so each possible combination of resource quantities has a 25% chance. Due to the uncertainty, there is no longer a single best plan but there is at least one optimal selection of construction options. The options with associated earliest expected completion times are:

(steel-frame, large-roof-panels)	21
(steel-frame, small-roof-panels)	22
(precast-frame, large-roof-panels)	21
(precast-frame, small-roof-panels)	22
(cast-in-place-frame, large-roof-panels)	22
(cast-in-place-frame, small-roof-panels)	23

In this case, the first and third options are both optimal.

10 Related Work

10.1 Theories of Objective Chance

Three outstanding subjective theories of objective chance are those of van Fraassen [68], Lewis [43], and Skyrms [63]. van Fraassen's model of objective chance is more constrained than Lewis's model which is more constrained than Skyrms's model. Thus, in van Fraassen's model, chance has more inherent properties than in either Lewis's or Skyrms's models. van Fraassen's theory is the only one of the three that is cast in a temporal framework.

van Fraassen. The model of objective chance used in $\mathcal{L}_{tca}$ is based on van Fraassen's [68] model of objective chance. He presents a semantic theory that models subjective probability and objective chance, using a future-branching model of time points. van Fraassen places two constraints on objective chance:

1. The chance of a past is either 0 or 1, depending on whether or not it actually occurred.
2. Chance at a time is completely determined by history of the world up to that time.

From these assumptions, he shows the following relation between subjective probability and objective chance

$$P_t(X|Y) = E_Y[C_t(X)],$$

where P_t is the subjective probability at time t, C_t is the objective chance at time t, E_Y is the expected value given Y, and provided the truth of Y depends only on the history up to t. This relation entails both Miller's principle and Lewis's principal principle, discussed below. Note that van Fraassen does not show that a similar relation holds between objective chances at different times, as does this monograph. In van Fraassen's models, objective chance can change with time but truth values cannot. He does not provide a logical language for his theory.

Lewis. Lewis's [43] theory of objective chance is based on his assertion that

... we have some very firm and definite opinions concerning reasonable credence *(subjective probability)* about chance *(objective chance)*. These opinions seem to me to afford the best grip we have on the concept of chance.

He describes a number of intuitive relationships between subjective probability and objective chance and shows that these are captured by his principal principle:

$$Pr(A|pr_t(A) = \alpha \wedge E) = \alpha,$$

where Pr is subjective probability, pr is objective chance, and E is any proposition compatible with $pr_t(A) = \alpha$ and admissible at time t.

The interesting thing here is the proposition E. The constraint that E be compatible with $pr_t(A) = \alpha$ means that $Pr(E \wedge pr_t(A) = \alpha) > 0$. Admissibility is less readily defined. Lewis does not give a definition of admissibility but he does characterize admissible propositions as "the sort of information whose impact on credence about outcomes comes entirely by way of credence about the chances of those outcomes." He gives two examples of admissible propositions. The first is historical information: "If a proposition is entirely about matters of fact at times no later than t, then as a rule that proposition is admissible." The other is hypothetical information about chance. By this he means conditionals where the consequent is a proposition about chance at a certain time and the antecedent is a proposition about history up to that time. So objective chance is invariant with respect to conditioning on admissible propositions. This concept of invariance under conditioning is the central notion of Brian Skyrms's theory of objective chance.

Skryms. Skyrms [63] works with the notion of resiliency. A probability value is resilient if it is relatively invariant under conditionalization over a set of sentences. The resiliency of $Pr(q)$ being α is defined as 1 minus the amplitude of the wiggle about α:

> The resiliency of $Pr(q)$ being α is $1 - \max|\alpha - Pr_j(q)|$ over $p_1, ..., p_n$, where the Pr_j's are gotten by conditionalizing on some Boolean combination of the p_i's which is logically consistent with q.

Skyrms then defines propensity (objective chance) as a highly resilient subjective probability. Of course, propensities will not be resilient over any partition. So a propensity will have a domain of resiliency. The chance of a penny coming up heads is $1/2$. This is invariant if we conditionalize on time, temperature, atmospheric pressure, etc. but not if we conditionalize on its being a biased coin.

Independent of his resiliency notion, Skyrms requires that propensities and subjective probabilities be related by Miller's principle:

$$Pr(A|pr(A) = \alpha) = \alpha,$$

where Pr is a subjective probability and pr is a propensity.

10.2 Temporal Probability Logics

The theory of computing literature contains several examples of logics that can represent both time and probability [42, 32, 28]. The focus of these logics is on reasoning about probabilistic programs and distributed systems. The logics do not attempt to model causality or to distinguish between different types of temporal objects such as facts and events; hence, they are not suitable for reasoning about actions and plans.

Kanazawa [37] presents a logic, $\mathcal{L}_{cp}$, of time and probability. The language allows quantification over time points but is propositional otherwise. The language contains a P operator for representing probability. The P operator is not temporally indexed so the language cannot represent the change of probability over time. Furthermore, the language does not allow nesting of probability operators. Like $\mathcal{L}_{tca}$, $\mathcal{L}_{cp}$ contains numeric functions for representing probability distributions. Because Kanazawa's focus is on representing the tendency of facts to persist through time, his representation of facts and events differs from ours. He describes a fact as "something that once it becomes true tends to stay true for some time." Facts are associated with temporal intervals. Events take place instantaneously and are associated with a single time point. He distinguishes three types of events. Persistence causation events are associated with a fact becoming true. Persistence termination events are associated with a fact becoming false. Point events are facts that stay true for only an instant. $\mathcal{L}_{cp}$ represents actions as events.

Kanazawa does not provide a detailed semantics for the language but mentions that the semantics will be given in [36] and sketches the model theory. Like the models for $\mathcal{L}_{tca}$, Kanazawa's models contain a collection of world-histories. He does not impose a branching time structure on the histories. The semantics of the P operator is defined in terms of probability distributions over world-histories. Fact tokens and event tokens are equated with (temporal interval, world) pairs. Kanazawa does not provide a proof theory for $\mathcal{L}_{cp}$.

Kanazawa goes on to describe his time net representation which is a kind of Bayes net that encodes the probability of facts and events over time. He states that the semantics of time nets is expressible within his logic but does not provide a specification. This idea of linking a graphic representation to a probability logic is similar to our use of $\mathcal{L}_{tca}$ to specify the semantics of the activity networks used in the cpm algorithm.

Dean and Wellman [12] present a propositional temporal probabilistic logic for representing planning problems. They extend Shoham's propositional temporal logic [61] by introducing a probability operator Pr. The temporal logic distinguishes liquid propositions, which if true over an interval are true over any subinterval, from event propositions which hold over the interval of the event's occurrence but over no proper subinterval. The language does not distinguish between actions and events. The probability operator cannot be nested but can otherwise be combined freely with other logical operators. The probability operator is not temporally indexed so the language cannot represent the change of probability over time. A model consists of a universe of time points, a set of possible time lines, a binary relation over time points, a discrete probability measure over the time lines, and an interpretation function. The models differ from those for $\mathcal{L}_{tca}$ by not imposing a branching structure on the time lines nor other constraints on the elements of the models. A sentence of the form $Pr(\phi) = \alpha$ is true if and only if the sum of the probabilities of the time lines in which ϕ is true is equal to α. A conditional probability sentence of the form $Pr(\phi_1|\phi_2) = \alpha$ is true if and only if the sum of the probabilities of the time lines in which $\phi_1 \wedge \phi_2$

is true divied by the sum of the probabilities of the time lines in which ϕ_2 is true is equal to α. They do not address the problem of conditioning on propositions of probability zero. They do not provide a proof theory.

10.3 Temporal Logics of Actions and Plans

Shoham [62] presents a branching time logic that formalizes the relation between time, knowledge, and action. Knowledge is defined in the standard way for modal logic and actions are defined as the ability to make choices among sets of world-histories. The model formalizes the notion that actions can only be performed under certain conditions. Shoham's logic does not capture the fact that actions cannot influence the past.

Pelavin [54, 52, 53] develops a future-branching time logic for reasoning about planning problems involving concurrent actions and external events. He starts with Allen's [1] linear temporal logic of time intervals and extends it with two modal operators, *INEV* and *IFTRIED*, to reason about future branching time and action effects, respectively. *INEV* is exactly our $\Box$ operator. *IFTRIED* is a counterfactual operator that associates the attempt of an action with the truth of a sentence. The semantics of the operator are based on Stalnaker's and Lewis's theories of counterfactuals. *IFTRIED* captures the temporal relation of action and effect—an action cannot affect the state of the world at any time preceding its attempt.

Pelavin does not distinguish between action types and action tokens. He represents actions and plans uniformly as "plan instances." A plan instance is an ordered pair: a set of basic action instances and a set of event instances, brought about by the basic actions. An action is attempted if its basic action instances occur and it occurs if its basic action instances and its event instances all occur. Since a plan instance is a single ordered pair and the times associated with the event and basic action instances are fixed and all terms in the language are rigid designators, a plan instance cannot occur more than once in a world history. If we want to allow two instances of the same plan to occur in a world history, they must have different names. Pelavin [52](p27) creates these different names by allowing an interval to be associated with a plan instance e.g. $pi@I$. This is to be interpreted as saying that plan instance pi occurs during interval I. But he does not provide a semantic definition for the @ operator to formalize the intuitive interpretation. Furthermore, by using different names for two occurrences of the same plan he has no way of saying that two instances of the *same* plan occur.

$\mathcal{L}_{tca}$ differs from Pelavin's logic in several other ways. Points are taken to be the primitive temporal objects rather than intervals. Pelavin [52](p84) himself notes that this results in a more natural definition of the accessibility relation. More importantly, $\mathcal{L}_{tca}$ can represent chance (desiderata point 1). Pelavin's logic, like ours, can represent incomplete information by saying, for example, that it is possible it will rain tomorrow and it is possible it will not. But his language cannot express that there is an 80% chance of rain tomorrow.

Conditional chance is used in this monograph to represent effects. Since chance can be conditioned on any sentence, $\mathcal{L}_{tca}$ can represent the effects of a wide variety of different phenomena. In Pelavin's logic, *IFTRIED* only associates effects with action attempts, so effects of general events cannot be represented. The use of conditional chance eliminates the need for a separate counterfactual operator and its semantic counterpart: the similarity measure over worlds. Furthermore, our representation of actions has a more intuitively appealing semantics. First, unlike Pelavin, we do not assume that actions are always feasible. Such an assumption is unacceptable since it is hard to imagine what it would mean for the basic action instances of two inconsistent actions, like concurrently remaining still and moving, to all occur.

Second, Pelavin's use of a Stalnaker/Lewis counterfactual operator to represent action effects results in some undesirable inferences. Consider the sentence "If I were to attempt to stay at home all day, then if I were to attempt to walk from home to the store at noon, I would succeed in walking from home to the store at noon." This sentence can be represented in Pelavin's logic by nesting two *IFTRIED* operators. If being at home is the executability condition for going from home to the store, Pelavin [52](p217) points out that the sentence is true in his logic. But attempting to stay home all day and attempting to go to the store at noon are incompatible. So it seems unreasonable for this sentence to be true in the intended interpretation[18]. It is true in Pelavin's logic because the semantics of the counterfactual is defined in terms of worlds that are similar up to the time of the action attempt. So the semantics allows everything about the world one is in after the time of the action attempt to be changed. In $\mathcal{L}_{tca}$ attempting to stay home all day and attempting to go the store at noon are incompatible, so their conjunction would not be feasible, and hence going to the store would have zero chance of occurring given that one was staying home all day.

Skyrms [63] provides an elegant probabilistic account of counterfactuals based on the notion of objective chance [Chap. IIA] and discusses the semantics of iterated probability conditionals [Appendix 3]. He shows that the iterated probability conditionals can lead to more intuitive inferences than iterated Stalnaker/Lewis conditionals.

---

[18] One might think that the sentence should be correct because going to the store is clipping staying at home, but the same problem arises if the temporal order of the actions is reversed.

11　Conclusions

This chapter summarizes the contributions of this monograph and discusses the limitations of the work, as well as directions for future research suggested by these limitations.

11.1　Summary

In Chap. 2, we presented the ontology of the logic. We specified the aspects of the world we intended to model, was well as their desired properties. Chapter 3 presented the syntax and semantics of the logic $\mathcal{L}_{tca}$. The desired intuitive properties outlined in the ontology were achieved by placing restrictions (C1) – (C8) on the models. A proof theory for the logic was presented in Chap. 4. The axioms and the theorems derivable in the proof theory serve to illustrate the properties embodied in the semantics.

In Chap. 5 we discussed how the logic can be used to describe properties of actions and plans. Actions and plans were characterized in terms of their feasibility, executability, and effects. Correspondingly, we identified three types of conditions that can influence actions: feasibility conditions, executability conditions, and ramification conditions. The concept of feasibility was defined in terms of choosability, which in turn was formalized using the logic's possibility modal operator. We showed that the logic's models of chance and possibility capture the temporal asymmetry between causes and effects.

Chapter 6 developed the concept of expected utility for acts that may not be feasible and discussed the relationship between goals and utilities. The expected utility of trying to attempt an act was shown to be a generalization of Jeffrey's concept of conditional expected utility. We specified conditions under which bounds on a plan's probability of achieving a goal delineate bounds on the plan's expected utility.

In Chap. 7 we showed how a planning problem can be described in terms of components: a goal description, a description of the planning environment, and specifications of the feasibility, executability, and effects of actions, in such a way that we can reason about the chance that a given plan will achieve the goal. We also showed how the logic can be used to represent action duration, the dependence of an action on resource availability, the degree of influence an action or event has over various conditions, and action interactions.

A specialized planning system for the problem of building construction planning was presented in Chap. 8. We demonstrated our proposed methodology for analysis and validation of planning algorithms by specifying the semantics of the system's data structures in terms of sentences in $\mathcal{L}_{tca}$ and by using this specification to prove correct a central component of the system.

11.2　Contributions

This monograph makes contributions to both Artificial Intelligence and Decision Theory. By drawing on the strength of previous work in both fields, we have been able to create a novel synthesis that addresses limitations of the traditional planning paradigm in each field. The contributions of the monograph fall into four main areas: the development of a vocabulary for describing planning problems, the development of a semantic theory that captures desired intuitive properties, the extension of the decision-theoretic framework to accommodate actions that may not be feasible, and the use of the decision-theoretic framework to provide a formal link between the representation of planning problems in the developed vocabulary and the concept of rationality.

Vocabulary. We have provided a vocabulary for describing planning problems involving time and chance. The richness of the vocabulary allows us to represent many of the central aspects of time and chance in planning. The language can express the chance of temporally qualified conditions in the world as well as the chance of action feasibility, executability, and effects. We can represent the extent to which conditions in the world can and cannot be influenced. This is an important capability since a planner must be able to reason about what conditions it can influence and the extent to which it can influence them. We can represent temporal aspects of plans such as concurrent actions and conditions during an action that influence its executability and effects. The language distinguishes between between actions and events. This distinction is important since an agent has much more direct control over its actions than over events. The language further distinguishes between action attempts and action occurrences. This distinction allows action duration to vary as a function of conditions in the world and it allows us to define the notion of action feasibility, the importance of which will be discussed below. The language allows first-order quantification over time points, probabilities, and domain individuals. This produces a language with great representational economy. For example, by quantifying over domain individuals we can describe classes of actions and by quantifying over time points we can describe states-of-affairs that are valid at each of some range of time points. No other currently existing logical language can represent these aspects of time and chance.

Semantic Theory. We have specified a set of constraints on the model theory that assigns meaning to the logical language. A constrained logic is desirable for several reasons. First, the more constrained the model theory, the greater the predictive power of the logic. In the extreme case, we could constrain the logic to allow only one model, thus giving us complete knowledge. But we do not want to over constrain the logic so that we eliminate models that are consistent with our conception of reality in the intended domains of applicability. Second, constraints provide guidance in assigning probabilities to sentences. This is an important function since the assigning of priors is a notoriously difficult task. So one would like a logic that is as constrained as possible yet does not produce unwanted inferences. The constraints we have imposed on the models capture numerous intuitive properties of time and chance in such a way that natural inferences follow directly from the semantics. For example, the following properties are a consequence of the constraints.

- The property that facts have higher chance of holding over their subintervals, (Theorem 23), is a consequence of semantic constraint (C3) and the definition of probability.
- The property that the past cannot be influenced (Axioms IT3 – IT6 and Theorems 31 – 37) follows from constraints (C1) and (C2) on the accessibility relation, constraint (C5) relating the accessibility relation to facts and events, and constraints (C6) and (C7) on probability.
- Millers' Principle (Axiom P3), which relates chance over time is a consequence of constraints (C6) and (C7). Furthermore, as a consequence of Miller's Principle we have the property that chance is the expected value of future chance, Theorem 19.
- The property that inevitability implies certainty (Axiom IP1):
  $$\Box_t \phi \rightarrow P_t(\phi) = 1$$
  follows from semantic constraints (C6) and (C7).

Feasibility. The integration of both chance and possibility in $\mathcal{L}_{tca}$ allowed us to define the notion of the chance of feasibility of an action or plan. This concept was then used to define the expected utility for actions that may not be feasible. This definition of expected utility is important in reasoning about plans for two reasons. First, it means that we can compute the expected utility of a partially specified plan since we no longer need to know what it means to execute the plan in all states of the world. Second, it means that we can reason about plans based on descriptions of individual actions since the definition of expected utility can encompass plans containing actions that interfere in such a way that their composition may not be feasible.

Rationality. Rationality, a central concept in Bayesian Decision Theory, has been notably lacking from the mainstream of work in AI. The application of this concept to planning systems is particularly important since the purpose of a planner is to choose a course of action, which we would like to know is rational in some well-defined sense. For practical reasons, planning systems in AI have traditionally planned to achieve symbolic goals. When cast in our framework, planning to achieve a goal becomes the task of choosing among plans with various chances of achieving the goal. The desire to retain the concept of a goal for its practical value required us to characterize planning to achieve goals in terms of rational choice.

We have developed the foundations for a theory of rationality in our logic by defining the concept of expected utility for the logic. Since the logic admits actions that might not be feasible, we needed to extend the decision-theoretic framework by defining the concept of expected utility for actions that may not be feasible – the expected utility of trying to attempt an action. We then generalized the traditional AI concept of goal and specified the relations that must hold between goals and utility functions so that the chance of a plan achieving a given goal can be used as a metric to gauge the expected utility of that plan.

The rationality of any given decision theory can be justified by two means. First, one can give examples of the choices recommended by the theory and argue that these are rational. We have provided a few examples to argue this but many more need to be worked through. Second, one can provide a representation theorem that derives the decision theory from constraints on more fundamental concepts. We have not provided a representation theorem for our decision theory. This is known in general to be a difficult problem. Some help on this problem might be obtained from work being done in Causal Decision Theory. Since our definition of objective chance is similar to that used in Causal Decision Theory, a representation theorem for Causal Decision Theory would likely provide guidance toward developing a representation theorem for our framework. The development of a representation theorem for Causal Decision Theory is the topic of active research.

11.3 Limitations and Future Research

Temporal Objects. In $\mathcal{L}_{tca}$ we have distinguished only three types of temporal objects: facts, events, and actions. Actions are composed of certain types of events. Facts are distinguished from events based on the relation between truth over an interval and truth over its subintervals. This same characterization can be used to distinguish many other types of temporal objects that are useful in planning. For example, one might like to define a *process* as roughly an event that occurs over its subintervals. This would allow us to more accurately represent processes like raining or falling. We might also wish to define the action analogue of processes such as walking or sleeping. Shoham [61] has identified ten different categories of temporal objects. Extending the present work to encompass Shoham's more refined categories is completely straightforward.

Subjective Probability. This paper has presented a logic for reasoning about objective chance. It is important for a planning representation to be able to represent the state of knowledge of the planning agent, e.g. to reason about actions that provide information, as well as the state of knowledge of other agents. This can be done by introducing subjective probabilities, which represent the beliefs of an agent, into the logic. Several philosophers have discussed the problem of combining subjective probability and objective chance [63, Appendix 2][43, 68]. The general consensus is that agents have subjective beliefs concerning objective chance and the two are related by certain constraints; although there is disagreement as to precisely what the constraints should be. It can be shown that such a hybrid representation of beliefs is necessary in order to make rational decisions in some cases where causality is a factor [63, ch IIC][44, 45]. Subjective probabilities are consistent with the present model theory. They can be modeled by defining probability functions over all worlds, not just the accessible ones. There would then be additional constraints on the models to relate subjective probabilities to objective chance.

Persistence. Notably lacking from the current framework is a theory of persistence. Persistence is the assumption that once some aspect of the world is in a certain state, it tends to remain in that state for some amount of time unless acted upon. Persistence plays an important role in reasoning about plans. In essence it tells us how rapidly the world changes so that the planning agent knows for how long its observations can be considered valid and consequently how often it needs to make new observations. Persistence is also important in reasoning about goals. In order to be able to plan to bring about a goal by sequentially bringing about its subgoals, an agent needs to know that once a subgoal is achieved, it will tend to remain true until the remaining subgoals are achieved. In the case of our construction planning system, we made this assumption implicitly and thus eliminated the necessity to reason about persistence.

Hanks [29, 31] and Dean and Kanazawa [9, 12] have both presented methods of formalizing persistence in a probabilistic setting. These approaches were discussed in Sect. 1.4. Persistence assumptions seem to be part of an agent's prior beliefs. These prior beliefs are updated upon making observations and upon committing to act. Thus the most appropriate method of modeling persistence in the present framework would be as constraints on an agent's subjective probabilities concerning objective chance. Persistence could be modeled as the decay of knowledge of objective chance over time.

Implementation. This monograph has focused primarily on formal aspects of the representation of planning problems. The implementation considerations discussed were limited to the particular problems that arise in the domain of construction planning. Since representation is a prerequisite to implementation, we now have a powerful tool to use in the formalization of planning problems and the development of suitable planning algorithms. Future work should address developing efficient algorithms that exploit the logic's ability to represent feasibility, executability, and effects of actions, as well as the logic's ability express statements that combine first-order quantification and probability.

Furthermore, we have only laid the theoretical groundwork for the incorporation of goals into a decision-theoretic planning framework. The desire to incorporate goals stems from their great practical value in the process of generating plans. We now need to build decision-theoretic planners that effectively use goals to gain efficiency.

Where do the Numbers Come From? One of the most often asked questions when someone presents a new representation formalism based on probabilities and utilities is "Where do the numbers come from?" Although this question is beyond the scope of this monograph, Decision Theory can provide some general answers. Much research has taken place on the problem of eliciting subjective probabilities [33, 59] as well as utilities [38] from human subjects. Values are elicited by observing a subject's choice behavior in controlled choice situations. The choice behavior can then be mapped to constraints on a probability and utility function via a representation theorem. So if we wish to be able to elicit probabilities from human subjects, the first step would be the development of a representation theorem. With such a tool in hand, one could draw on the techniques developed for other decision theories. But even with a formal framework in place, probabilities and utilities are notoriously difficult to assess.

The area of multi-attribute utility theory [38] addresses the issue of effectively eliciting a utility function by decomposing it into component functions. Recent work in AI [26, 25, 72, 77] addresses the relationship between goals and utilities. This work attempts to place constraints on the form of utility functions in order to facilitate elicitation and to allow the utility functions to be used to guide the process of plan generation in the same way that goals are used.

A Soundness Proofs

We prove the soundness of the more intersting and less commonly known of the axioms in Chap. 4. The first few proofs we present in detail. The remaining proofs are presented less formally.

I1) $\Box_t\phi \to \phi$

Proof. We prove this sentence valid by showing that it is satisfied by an arbitrary model M, world w, and assignment function $g[d/t]$. By the semantic definitions, $[\![\Box_t\phi \to \phi]\!]^{M,w,g[d/t]} = \text{true}$ iff $[\![\neg\Box_t\phi]\!]^{M,w,g[d/t]} = \text{true}$ or $[\![\phi]\!]^{M,w,g[d/t]} = \text{true}$. The first disjunct is true iff for some w' such that $R(d,w,w')$ $[\![\phi]\!]^{M,w',g[d/t]} = \text{false}$. If this is not the case then ϕ is true in all worlds w' such that $R(d,w,w')$. And since by (C2) $R(d,w,w)$, it follows that ϕ is true in w. $\qquad\square$

I2) $\Box_t(\phi \to \psi) \to (\Box_t\phi \to \Box_t\psi)$

Proof. By the semantic definitions, $[\![\Box_t(\phi \to \psi) \to (\Box_t\phi \to \Box_t\psi)]\!]^{M,w,g[d/t]} = \text{true}$ iff $[\![\neg\Box_t(\phi \to \psi)]\!]^{M,w,g[d/t]} = \text{true}$ or $[\![\Box_t\phi \to \Box_t\psi]\!]^{M,w,g[d/t]} = \text{true}$. By the semantic definitions, this is true iff $[\![\Box_t\phi \wedge \neg\psi]\!]^{M,w,g[d/t]} = \text{false}$ or $[\![\Diamond_t\phi]\!]^{M,w,g[d/t]} = \text{true}$ or $[\![\Box_t\psi]\!]^{M,w,g[d/t]} = \text{true}$. If the first disjunct is not the case then in every world we have $\neg\phi \vee \psi$. So in every world ϕ is false or ψ is true. If ϕ is false in some world, the second disjunct is satisfied and we're done. Otherwise, ψ must be true in every world, in which case the third disjunct is satisfied. $\qquad\square$

I3) $\Box_t\phi \to \Box_t\Box_t\phi$

Proof. By the semantic definitions, $[\![\Box_t\phi \to \Box_t\Box_t\phi]\!]^{M,w,g[d/t]} = \text{true}$ iff $[\![\Box_t\phi]\!]^{M,w,g[d/t]} = \text{false}$ or $[\![\Box_t\Box_t\phi]\!]^{M,w,g[d/t]} = \text{true}$. If the first disjunct is not the case then ϕ is true in all worlds w' such that $R(d,w,w')$. Now $[\![\Box_t\Box_t\phi]\!]^{M,w,g[d/t]} = \text{true}$ iff $[\![\phi]\!]^{M,w,g[d/t]} = \text{true}$ for all w'' such that $R(d,w',w'')$ and $R(d,w,w')$. But by (C2) this is true iff $[\![\phi]\!]^{M,w,g[d/t]} = \text{true}$ for all w' such that $R(d,w,w')$. $\qquad\square$

I4) $\Diamond_t\phi \to \Box_t\Diamond_t\phi$

Proof. By the semantic definitions and the definition of possibility, $[\![\Diamond_t\phi \to \Box_t\Diamond_t\phi]\!]^{M,w,g[d/t]} = \text{true}$ iff $[\![\Box_t\neg\phi]\!]^{M,w,g[d/t]} = \text{true}$ or $[\![\Box_t\Diamond_t\phi]\!]^{M,w,g[d/t]} = \text{true}$. If the first disjunct is not the case then ϕ is true in some world w° such that $R(d,w,w^\circ)$. Now $[\![\Box_t\Diamond_t\phi]\!]^{M,w,g[d/t]} = \text{true}$ iff for every world w' such that $R(d,w,w')$ there exists a world w'' such that $R(d,w,w'')$ and $[\![\phi]\!]^{M,w,g[d/t]} = \text{true}$. But by (C2) $R(d,w,w^\circ)$ and $R(d,w,w')$ implies $R(d,w',w^\circ)$. So w° is the required world w''. $\qquad\square$

NEC) Rule of Necessitation
   From ϕ infer $\square_t\phi$.

Proof. $[\![\square_t\phi]\!]^{M,w,g} = $ true iff $[\![\phi]\!]M, w', g[d/t] = $ true for all w' such that $R(d, w, w')$. By definition, if ϕ is valid then $[\![\phi]\!]^{M,w,g} = $ true for all M, w, g. $\square$

P3) Miller's Principle

$$(t_1 \preceq t_2) \;\rightarrow\; P_{t_1}(\phi \mid P_{t_2}(\phi) \geq \alpha) \geq \alpha$$

Proof. We first prove an expected value property and then use it to prove Miller's principle. Let t, t' be two time points $t \leq t'$ and consider the R-equivalence classes of worlds at time t'. Let the variable r range over these equivalence classes. The r form a partition of W, so the probability of a set X can be written as the integral over this partition:

$$\mu_t^w(X) = \int_{r \subset W} \mu_t^w(X|r)\mu_t^w(dr)$$

Since the history up to time t' determines the probability at time t', this can be written as

$$\mu_t^w(X) = \int_{r \subset W} \mu_{t'}^r(X)\mu_t^w(dr),$$

where $\mu_{t'}^r$ denotes the probability at time t' in equivalence class r. Since the probability at a given time is assumed to be constant over all worlds in an R-equivalence class, the probability at a given time is the expected value of the probability at any future time:

$$\mu_t^w(X) = \int_W \mu_{t'}^{w'}(X)\mu_t^w(dw').$$

Next we show that Miller's principle is valid in the probability models. By the expected value property,

$$\mu_t^w(X \cap \{w' : \mu_{t'}^{w'}(X) = \alpha\}) =$$
$$\int_W \mu_{t'}^{w''}(X \cap \{w' : \mu_{t'}^{w'}(X) = \alpha\})\mu_t^w(dw'').$$

Now, by semantic constraints (C6) and (C7) it follows that

$$\forall w \in \{w' : \mu_{t'}^{w'}(X) = \alpha\}, \; \mu_{t'}^w(\{w' : \mu_{t'}^{w'}(X) = \alpha\}) = 1$$
$$\forall w \notin \{w' : \mu_{t'}^{w'}(X) = \alpha\}, \; \mu_{t'}^w(\{w' : \mu_{t'}^{w'}(X) = \alpha\}) = 0.$$

So we can restrict the integral to the set
$\{w' : \mu_{t'}^{w'}(X) = \alpha\}$:

$$= \int_{\{w' : \mu_{t'}^{w'}(X) = \alpha\}} \mu_{t'}^{w''}(X \cap \{w' : \mu_{t'}^{w'}(X) = \alpha\})\mu_t^w(dw'').$$

And by the above property again
$\mu_{t'}^{w''}(X \cap \{w' : \mu_{t'}^{w'}(X) = \alpha\}) = \alpha$, so

$$= \alpha \cdot \int_{\{w' : \mu_{t'}^{w'}(X) = \alpha\}} \mu_t^w(dw'').$$

$$= \alpha \cdot \mu_t^w(\{w' : \mu_{t'}^{w'}(X) = \alpha\}).$$

By the semantic definitions it follows that

$$P_t(\phi \wedge P_{t'}(\phi) = \alpha) = \alpha \cdot P_t(P_{t'}(\phi) = \alpha).$$

And by a slight generalization of the proof it follows that

$$\forall (t \preceq t') \; P_t(\phi \wedge P_{t'}(\phi) \geq \alpha) \geq \alpha \cdot P_t(P_{t'}(\phi) \geq \alpha).$$

$\square$

TL1) Facts hold over their sub-intervals.

$$(t_1 \preceq t_2 \preceq t_3 \preceq t_4) \wedge (t_1 \neq t_3) \wedge (t_2 \neq t_4) \rightarrow$$
$$[HOLDS(FA, t_1, t_4) \rightarrow HOLDS(FA, t_2, t_3)]$$

Proof. This follows directly from constraint (C3).

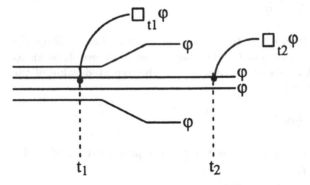

Fig. 29. Model for the proof that inevitability persists.

IT1) Inevitability persists

$$(t_1 \preceq t_2) \rightarrow (\Box_{t_1} \phi \rightarrow \Box_{t_2} \phi)$$

Proof. The model described in the proof is shown in Fig. 29.
$[\![\Box_{t_1}(\phi)]\!]^{M,w',g[d_1/t_1,d_2/t_2]} = $ true iff for all w' such that
$R(d_1, w, w')$ $[\![\phi]\!]^{M,w',g[d_1/t_1,d_2/t_2]} = $ true. Now suppose that for some w'' such that
$R(d_2, w, w'')$, $[\![\phi]\!]^{M,w'',g[d_1/t_1,d_2/t_2]} = $ false. Then by (C1), $R(d_1, w, w'')$. This is a
contradiction. So for all w'' such that $R(d_2, w, w'')$, $[\![\phi]\!]^{M,w'',g[d_1/t_1,d_2/t_2]} = $ true.

$\square$

IT3) Past facts are inevitable.

$$(t_0 \preceq t_1 \preceq t_2) \rightarrow [\Box_{t_2} HOLDS(Q, t_0, t_1) \vee \Box_{t_2} \neg HOLDS(Q, t_0, t_1)]$$

Proof.

$[\Box_{t_2} HOLDS(Q, t_0, t_1) \vee \Box_{t_2} \neg HOLDS(Q, t_0, t_1)]^{M,w,g[d_0/t_0,d_1/t_1,d_2/t_2]}$ = true iff
$[HOLDS(Q, t_0, t_1)]^{M,w',g[d_0/t_0,d_1/t_1,d_2/t_2]}$ = true for all w' such that $R(d_2, w, w')$
or
$[HOLDS(Q, t_0, t_1)]^{M,w',g[d_0/t_0,d_1/t_1,d_2/t_2]}$ = false for all w' such that $R(d_2, w, w')$.
This is the case iff
$\langle (d_0, d_1), w' \rangle \in F(Q)$ for all w' such that $R(d_2, w, w')$ or
$\langle (d_0, d_1), w' \rangle \notin F(Q)$ for all w' such that $R(d_2, w, w')$.
This last statment follows directly from (C5). □

IP1) Inevitability implies certainty

$$\Box_t(\phi) \rightarrow P_t(\phi) = 1$$

Proof. We prove this sentence valid by showing that it is satisfied by an arbitrary
model M, world w, and assignment function $g[d/t]$. By the semantic definitions,
$[\Box_t(\phi) \rightarrow P_t(\phi) = 1]^{M,w,g[d/t]}$ = true iff $[\Diamond_t(\neg\phi)]^{M,w,g[d/t]}$ = true or
$[P_t(\phi) = 1]^{M,w,g[d/t]}$ = true. The first disjunct holds if for some w' such that
$R(d, w, w')$ $[\phi]^{M,w',g[d/t]}$ = false. If this is not the case then $[\phi]^{M,w',g[d/t]}$ = true
for all w' such that $R(d, w, w')$.
So $R_d^w \subseteq \{w' : [\phi]^{M,w,g[d/t]}$ = true$\}$. But by Meta-Theorem 2, $\mu_d^w(R_d^w) = 1$.
So $\mu_d^w(\{w' : [\phi]^{M,w',g[d/t]}$ = true$\}) = 1$.
And from the semantic definitions it follows that $[P_t(\phi) = 1]^{M,w,g[d/t]}$ = true. □

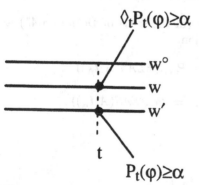

Fig. 30. Model for the proof that current chance is inevitable.

IP2) Current chance is inevitable.

$$\Diamond_t P_t(\phi) \geq \alpha \rightarrow \Box_t P_t(\phi) \geq \alpha$$

Proof. The model described in the proof is shown in Fig. 30.
$[\![\Diamond_t P_t(\phi) \geq \alpha]\!]^{M,w,g[d/t]} = \text{true}$ iff $[\![P_t(\phi) \geq \alpha]\!]^{M,w,g[d/t]} = \text{true}$ for some w' such that $R(d, w, w')$. This is the case iff $\mu_d^{w'}(\{w'' : [\![\phi]\!]^{M,w'',g[d/t]} = \text{true}\}) \geq \alpha$ for some w' such that $R(d, w, w')$. Choose an arbitrary w° such that $R(d, w, w^\circ)$. By (C2), $R(d, w', w^\circ)$. Hence by (C6), $\mu_d^{w^\circ}((\{w'' : [\![\phi]\!]^{M,w'',g[d/t]} = \text{true}\}) \geq \alpha$.

$\Box$

B Development of Action Feasibility

We wish to show that the chance that an action is feasible $P_t(FEAS(A, t_A))$ is equal to the chance that it is attempted given that the agent tries to attempt it. To show this equivalence, we need to introduce an new predicate into the language. $TATT(A, t_A)$ is true if an agent tries to attempt action A at time t_A. One can think of trying to attempt an action at a time t_A as mentally committing at some time before t_A to attempting the action at t_A. Trying to attempt an action is something an agent can always do. For the purposes of the proof, it will suffice to characterize $TATT$ in terms of its relation to action attempts and feasibility. The relation is captured by two assumptions:

FA1) Trying to attempt an action results in the action's attempt if the action is feasible (in the sense of Definition 45).

$$P_{now}(ATT(A, t_A) \mid FEAS(A, t_A) \land TATT(A, t_A)) = 1$$

FA2) The chance of feasibility of an action (in the sense of Definition 45) is independent of trying to attempt the action.

$$P_{now}(FEAS(A, t_A) \mid TATT(A, t_A)) = P_{now}(FEAS(A, t_A))$$

Theorem 51. $P_t(ATT(A, t_A) \mid TATT(A, t_A)) = P_t(FEAS(A, t_A))$

By Axiom P2,

$$P_t(ATT(A, t_A) \mid TATT(A, t_A)) =$$
$$P_t(ATT(A, t_A) \land FEAS(A, t_A) \mid TATT(A, t_A)) +$$
$$P_t(ATT(A, t_A) \land \neg FEAS(A, t_A) \mid TATT(A, t_A))$$

By Theorem 43,

$$P_t(ATT(A, t_A) \mid TATT(A, t_A)) =$$
$$P_t(ATT(A, t_A) \land FEAS(A, t_A) \mid TATT(A, t_A))$$

By the definition of conditional probability,

$$P_t(ATT(A, t_A) \mid TATT(A, t_A)) =$$
$$P_t(ATT(A, t_A) \mid FEAS(A, t_A) \wedge TATT(A, t_A)) \cdot$$
$$P_t(FEAS(A, t_A) \mid TATT(A, t_A))$$

By assumption FA1,

$$P_t(ATT(A, t_A) \mid TATT(A, t_A)) = 1 \cdot P_t(FEAS(A, t_A) \mid TATT(A, t_A))$$

Finally by assumption FA2,

$$P_t(ATT(A, t_A) \mid TATT(A, t_A)) = P_t(FEAS(A, t_A))$$

□

C   Derivation of the Chance of Plan Feasibility

We wish to derive an expression for the chance that a plan is feasibile using only the notions of action attempts and the feasibility of single actions. We derive the expression for a plan consisting of only two actions and then generalize to an arbitrary number of actions. Consider the plan consisting of the two action attempts $ATT(A_1, t_{A_1})$ and $ATT(A_2, t_{A_2})$. The chance that this plan is feasible is

$$P_{now}(ATT(A_1, t_{A_1}) \wedge ATT(A_2, t_{A_2}) \mid TATT(A_1, t_{A_1}) \wedge TATT(A_2, t_{A_2}))$$

Suppose first that $t_{A_1} = t_{A_2}$. In this case, the attempt of the plan is just equivalent to the attempt of a single more complex action. So

$$P_{now}(ATT(A_1, t_{A_1}) \wedge ATT(A_2, t_{A_2}) \mid \tag{112}$$
$$TATT(A_1, t_{A_1}) \wedge TATT(A_2, t_{A_2})) = P_{now}(FEAS(\{A_1, A_2\}, t_{A_1}))$$

Now suppose that A_1 may also preceed A_2, i.e., $t_{A_1} \leq t_{A_2}$. We make three assumptions.

FA3) Actions are volitional.

$$ATT(A, t_A) \rightarrow TATT(A, t_A)$$

This assumption is consistent with the task of planning courses of action. It would not make sense to plan to directly attempt non-volitional actions. For example, I cannot plan to directly sneeze unintentionally; on the other hand, I can plan to put pepper under my nose to make myself sneeze unintentionally. In this case putting the pepper under my nose is the action I plan and sneezing is an effect of the action.

FA4) The chance that an action is feasible is independent of trying to attempt the action and any other concurrent or later actions.

$$P_{now}(FEAS(A_1, t_{A_1}) \mid TATT(A_1, t_{A_1}) \wedge TATT(A_2, t_{A_2})) =$$
$$P_{now}(FEAS(A_1, t_{A_1}))$$

FA5) The chance that an action is feasible is independent of trying to attemt the act, in the context of an earlier action attempt.

$$P_{now}(FEAS(A_2, t_{A_2})|ATT(A_1, t_{A_1}) \wedge TATT(A_2, t_{A_2})) =$$
$$P_{now}(FEAS(A_2, t_{A_2})|ATT(A_1, t_{A_1}))$$

By the definition of conditional probability, the chance that the plan consisting of $ATT(A_1, t_{A_1})$ and $ATT(A_2, t_{A_2})$ is feasible is

$$P_{now}(ATT(A_1, t_{A_1}) \wedge ATT(A_2, t_{A_2})| \qquad (113)$$
$$TATT(A_1, t_{A_1}) \wedge TATT(A_2, t_{A_2})) =$$
$$P_{now}(ATT(A_2, t_{A_2})|ATT(A_1, t_{A_1}) \wedge TATT(A_1, t_{A_1}) \wedge TATT(A_2, t_{A_2})) \cdot$$
$$P_{now}(ATT(A_1, t_{A_1})|TATT(A_1, t_{A_1}) \wedge TATT(A_2, t_{A_2}))$$

By assumption FA3, the first term in (113) can be written as

$$P_{now}(ATT(A_2, t_{A_2})| \qquad (114)$$
$$ATT(A_1, t_{A_1}) \wedge TATT(A_1, t_{A_1}) \wedge TATT(A_2, t_{A_2})) =$$
$$P_{now}(ATT(A_2, t_{A_2})|ATT(A_1, t_{A_1}) \wedge TATT(A_2, t_{A_2}))$$

which by Theorem 43 is just

$$= P_{now}(ATT(A_2, t_{A_2}) \wedge FEAS(A_2, t_{A_2})| \qquad (115)$$
$$ATT(A_1, t_{A_1}) \wedge TATT(A_2, t_{A_2}))$$

By the definition of conditional probability, this may be written as

$$= P_{now}(ATT(A_2, t_{A_2})| \qquad (116)$$
$$FEAS(A_2, t_{A_2}) \wedge ATT(A_1, t_{A_1}) \wedge TATT(A_2, t_{A_2})) \cdot$$
$$P_{now}(FEAS(A_2, t_{A_2})|ATT(A_1, t_{A_1}) \wedge TATT(A_2, t_{A_2}))$$

By assumption FA1, the first term is just one:

$$= (1) \cdot P_{now}(FEAS(A_2, t_{A_2})|ATT(A_1, t_{A_1}) \wedge TATT(A_2, t_{A_2})) \qquad (117)$$

And by assumption FA5, we have

$$= P_{now}(FEAS(A_2, t_{A_2})|ATT(A_1, t_{A_1})) \qquad (118)$$

Now by Theorem 43 the second term in (113) can be written as

$$P_{now}(ATT(A_1, t_{A_1})|TATT(A_1, t_{A_1}) \wedge TATT(A_2, t_{A_2})) = \qquad (119)$$
$$P_{now}(ATT(A_1, t_{A_1}) \wedge FEAS(A_1, t_{A_1})|$$
$$TATT(A_1, t_{A_1}) \wedge TATT(A_2, t_{A_2}))$$

By the definition of conditional probability, this may be written as

$$= P_{now}(ATT(A_1, t_{A_1})| \qquad (120)$$
$$FEAS(A_1, t_{A_1}) \wedge TATT(A_1, t_{A_1}) \wedge TATT(A_2, t_{A_2})) \cdot$$
$$P_{now}(FEAS(A_1, t_{A_1})|TATT(A_1, t_{A_1}) \wedge TATT(A_2, t_{A_2}))$$

By assumption FA1, the first term is just one:

$$= (1) \cdot P_{now}(FEAS(A_1, t_{A_1}) \mid TATT(A_1, t_{A_1}) \wedge TATT(A_2, t_{A_2})) \tag{121}$$

Any by assumption FA4 we have

$$= P_{now}(FEAS(A_1, t_{A_1})) \tag{122}$$

So substituting back into (113) we get

$$P_{now}(ATT(A_1, t_{A_1}) \wedge ATT(A_2, t_{A_2}) \mid \tag{123}$$
$$TATT(A_1, t_{A_1}) \wedge TATT(A_2, t_{A_2})) =$$
$$P_{now}(FEAS(A_2, t_{A_2}) \mid ATT(A_1, t_{A_1})) \cdot P_{now}(FEAS(A_1, t_{A_1}))$$

In general, for a plan with n actions such that $t_{A_1} \leq t_{A_2} \leq ... \leq t_{A_n}$ we have that

$$P_{now}(\wedge_i ATT(A_i, t_{A_i}) \mid \wedge_i TATT(A_i, t_{A_i})) = \tag{124}$$
$$\prod_{i=1}^{n} P_{now}(FEAS(A_i, t_{A_i}) \mid \wedge_{j<i} ATT(A_j, t_{A_j}))$$

Notice that from (123) and (112) it follows that for $t_{A_1} = t_{A_2}$ we have

$$P_{now}(FEAS(\{A_1, A_2\}, t_{A_1}) = \tag{125}$$
$$P_{now}(FEAS(A_2, t_{A_2}) \mid ATT(A_1, t_{A_1})) \cdot P_{now}(FEAS(A_1, t_{A_1}))$$

D Derivation of EUT

We wish to derive an expression for the expected utility of trying to attempt an action from Jeffrey's definition of conditional expected utility. We do this using the predicate $TATT$. The derivation requires assumptions FA1 and FA2 from Appendix B and FA3 from Appendix C. By definition, the conditional expected utility of trying to attempt an action A at time t_A is

$$\mathbf{CEU}(TATT(A, t_A)) = \sum_{w \in W} P_t(w \mid TATT(A, t_A)) \cdot \mathbf{U}(w) \tag{126}$$

By Axiom P2, this can be written as

$$\mathbf{CEU}(TATT(A, t_A)) = \tag{127}$$
$$\sum_{w \in W} [P_t(w \wedge ATT(A, t_A) \wedge FEAS(A, t_A) \mid TATT(A, t_A)) +$$
$$P_t(w \wedge \neg ATT(A, t_A) \wedge FEAS(A, t_A) \mid TATT(A, t_A)) +$$
$$P_t(w \wedge ATT(A, t_A) \wedge \neg FEAS(A, t_A) \mid TATT(A, t_A)) +$$
$$P_t(w \wedge \neg ATT(A, t_A) \wedge \neg FEAS(A, t_A) \mid TATT(A, t_A))] \cdot \mathbf{U}(w)$$

Now, by Axiom P2 (or alternatively by the relation between attempt and feasibility), the second half of expression (127) may be rewritten as

$$P_t(w \wedge ATT(A, t_A) \wedge \neg FEAS(A, t_A) \mid TATT(A, t_A)) +$$
$$P_t(w \wedge \neg ATT(A, t_A) \wedge \neg FEAS(A, t_A) \mid TATT(A, t_A)) =$$
$$P_t(w \wedge \neg FEAS(A, t_A) \mid TATT(A, t_A)) \tag{128}$$

By assumption FA2,

$$= P_t(w \mid \neg FEAS(A, t_A) \land TATT(A, t_A)) \cdot P_t(\neg FEAS(A, t_A)) \tag{129}$$

Now, the first term in expression (127) may be written as

$$P_t(w \land ATT(A, t_A) \land FEAS(A, t_A) \mid TATT(A, t_A)) =$$
$$P_t(w \mid ATT(A, t_A) \land FEAS(A, t_A) \land TATT(A, t_A)) \cdot$$
$$P_t(ATT(A, t_A) \land FEAS(A, t_A) \mid TATT(A, t_A)) \tag{130}$$

Since by Theorem 43 $ATT(A, t_A) \to FEAS(A, t_A)$, the first term in (130) may be written as[19]

$$P_t(w \mid ATT(A, t_A) \land FEAS(A, t_A) \land TATT(A, t_A)) =$$
$$P_t(w \mid ATT(A, t_A) \land TATT(A, t_A)) \tag{131}$$

And since we have assumed that actions are volitional FA3,

$$= P_t(w \mid ATT(A, t_A)) \tag{132}$$

The second term in (130) may be written as

$$P_t(ATT(A, t_A) \land FEAS(A, t_A) \mid TATT(A, t_A)) =$$
$$P_t(ATT(A, t_A) \mid FEAS(A, t_A) \land TATT(A, t_A)) \cdot$$
$$P_t(FEAS(A, t_A) \mid TATT(A, t_A)) \tag{133}$$

By FA1,
$$= P_t(FEAS(A, t_A) \mid TATT(A, t_A)) \tag{134}$$

And by the independence assumption FA2,[20]

$$= P_t(FEAS(A, t_A)) \tag{135}$$

Now expressions (132) and (135) can be substituted back into (130) to yield

$$P_t(w \land ATT(A, t_A) \land FEAS(A, t_A) \mid TATT(A, t_A)) =$$
$$P_t(w \mid ATT(A, t_A)) \cdot P_t(FEAS(A, t_A)) \tag{136}$$

Finally we simplify the second term in the expected utility expression (127).

$$P_t(w \land \neg ATT(A, t_A) \land FEAS(A, t_A) \mid TATT(A, t_A)) =$$
$$P_t(w \mid \neg ATT(A, t_A) \land FEAS(A, t_A) \land TATT(A, t_A)) \cdot$$
$$P_t(\neg ATT(A, t_A) \land FEAS(A, t_A) \mid TATT(A, t_A)) \tag{137}$$

---

[19] Notice that defining feasibility as $FEAS(A, t_A)$ is absolutely crucial to this derivation. If it were defined as $P_{t_A}(ATT(A, t_A)) > 0$, the derivation would not go through.

[20] It follows from this by Theorem 43 that $P_t(FEAS(A, t_A)) = P_t(ATT(A, t_A) \mid TATT(A, t_A))$.

Now, the second term in (137) can be rewritten as

$$P_t(\neg ATT(A, t_A) \wedge FEAS(A, t_A) \mid TATT(A, t_A)) =$$
$$P_t(\neg ATT(A, t_A) \mid FEAS(A, t_A) \wedge TATT(A, t_A)) \cdot$$
$$P_t(FEAS(A, t_A) \mid TATT(A, t_A)) \tag{138}$$

By FA1 the first term in (138) is just 0, so

$$P_t(w \wedge \neg ATT(A, t_A) \wedge FEAS(A, t_A) \mid TATT(A, t_A)) = 0 \tag{139}$$

Now, substituting expressions (129) (136) (139) back into the expression (127) for conditional expected utility yields[21]

$$\mathbf{CEU}(TATT(A, t_A)) = \sum_{w \in W} [P_t(w \mid ATT(A, t_A)) \cdot P_t(FEAS(A, t_A)) +$$
$$P_t(w \mid \neg FEAS(A, t_A) \wedge TATT(A, t_A)) \cdot$$
$$P_t(\neg FEAS(A, t_A))] \cdot \mathbf{U}(w) \tag{140}$$

We will refer to this as the expected utility at time t of trying to attempt action A at time t_A and write it as $\mathbf{EUT}(ATT(A, t_A), t)$. When the action is certainly feasible, this reduces to the standard conditional expected utility of attempting the action:

$$EUT(ATT(A, t_A), t) = \sum_{w \in W} P_t(w \mid ATT(A, t_A)) \cdot \mathbf{U}(w) \tag{141}$$

This makes good intuitive sense since if the action is feasible then trying to attempt the action will always result in its being attempted.

E   Derivation of the Chance that Trying to Attempt a Plan Achieves a Given Goal

We wish to derive an expression for the chance that trying to attempt a plan achieves a given goal in which the predicate $TATT$ does not appear. We first derive an expression for a plan consisting of only two actions and then generalize to an arbitrary number of actions.

The chance that trying to attempt the plan consisting of action attempts $ATT(A_1, t_{A_1})$ and $ATT(A_2, t_{A_2})$ achieves goal G is

$$P_{now}(G \mid TATT(A_1, t_{A_1}) \wedge TATT(A_2, t_{A_2}))$$

---

[21] This definition of expected utility applies just as well to acts for which we do not distinguish between attempt and occurrence. In this case the expression would represent the expected utility of trying to *execute* the action.

Suppose, without loss of generality, that $t_{A_1} \leq t_{A_2}$. By Axiom P2,

$$P_{now}(G \mid TATT(A_1, t_{A_1}) \wedge TATT(A_2, t_{A_2})) = \tag{142}$$
$$P_{now}(G \wedge ATT(A_1, t_{A_1}) \wedge ATT(A_2, t_{A_2}) \wedge$$
$$FEAS(A_1, t_{A_1}) \wedge FEAS(A_2, t_{A_2}) \mid TATT(A_1, t_{A_1}) \wedge TATT(A_2, t_{A_2})) +$$
$$P_{now}(G \wedge \neg ATT(A_1, t_{A_1}) \wedge ATT(A_2, t_{A_2}) \wedge$$
$$\neg FEAS(A_1, t_{A_1}) \wedge FEAS(A_2, t_{A_2}) \mid TATT(A_1, t_{A_1}) \wedge TATT(A_2, t_{A_2})) +$$
$$P_{now}(G \wedge ATT(A_1, t_{A_1}) \wedge \neg ATT(A_2, t_{A_2}) \wedge$$
$$FEAS(A_1, t_{A_1}) \wedge \neg FEAS(A_2, t_{A_2}) \mid TATT(A_1, t_{A_1}) \wedge TATT(A_2, t_{A_2})) +$$
$$P_{now}(G \wedge \neg ATT(A_1, t_{A_1}) \wedge \neg ATT(A_2, t_{A_2}) \wedge$$
$$\neg FEAS(A_1, t_{A_1}) \wedge \neg FEAS(A_2, t_{A_2}) \mid TATT(A_1, t_{A_1}) \wedge TATT(A_2, t_{A_2})) +$$
$$\mathcal{T}$$

The symbol $\mathcal{T}$ represents twelve terms in which the polarity of at least one of the $ATT(A_i, t_{A_i})$, $FEAS(A_i, t_{A_i})$ pairs disagrees, i.e., the term contains either $ATT(A_i, t_{A_i}) \wedge \neg FEAS(A_i, t_{A_i})$ or $\neg ATT(A_i, t_{A_i}) \wedge FEAS(A_i, t_{A_i})$. In the first case, the probability of the term is zero since by Theorem 43 $\neg FEAS(A_i, t_{A_i}) \rightarrow \neg ATT(A_i, t_{A_i})$. In the second case, the term can be written, for example, as

$$P_{now}(G \wedge \neg ATT(A_1, t_{A_1}) \wedge ATT(A_2, t_{A_2}) \wedge \tag{143}$$
$$FEAS(A_1, t_{A_1}) \wedge FEAS(A_2, t_{A_2}) \mid TATT(A_1, t_{A_1}) \wedge TATT(A_2, t_{A_2})) =$$
$$P_{now}(\neg ATT(A_1, t_{A_1}) \mid G \wedge ATT(A_2, t_{A_2}) \wedge FEAS(A_1, t_{A_1}) \wedge FEAS(A_2, t_{A_2})$$
$$\wedge TATT(A_1, t_{A_1}) \wedge TATT(A_2, t_{A_2})) \cdot$$
$$P_{now}(G \wedge ATT(A_2, t_{A_2}) \wedge FEAS(A_1, t_{A_1}) \wedge FEAS(A_2, t_{A_2}) \mid$$
$$TATT(A_1, t_{A_1}) \wedge TATT(A_2, t_{A_2}))$$

Now, by assumption FA1 the second term in this expression is just zero. Hence, all terms represented by $\mathcal{T}$ are zero terms.

Since by Theorem 43 $ATT(A_i, t_{A_i}) \rightarrow FEAS(A_i, t_{A_i})$, the first term in (142) may be written

$$P_{now}(G \wedge ATT(A_1, t_{A_1}) \wedge ATT(A_2, t_{A_2}) \mid \tag{144}$$
$$TATT(A_1, t_{A_1}) \wedge TATT(A_2, t_{A_2})) =$$
$$P_{now}(G \mid ATT(A_1, t_{A_1}) \wedge ATT(A_2, t_{A_2})) \cdot$$
$$P_{now}(ATT(A_1, t_{A_1}) \wedge ATT(A_2, t_{A_2}) \mid TATT(A_1, t_{A_1}) \wedge TATT(A_2, t_{A_2}))$$

The second term in (144) is just the expression for plan feasibility, so the expression is just

$$= P_{now}(G \mid ATT(A_1, t_{A_1}) \wedge ATT(A_2, t_{A_2})) \cdot \tag{145}$$
$$P_{now}(FEAS(A_2, t_{A_2}) \mid ATT(A_1, t_{A_1})) \cdot P_{now}(FEAS(A_1, t_{A_1}))$$

The remaining three terms in (142) represent the chance that the goal will come about if one or both of the actions are not attempted. Each of these terms may be positive. So, if we are reasoning about the chance that the goal is achieved simply through trying to attempt the plan, regardless of whether the plan actually occurs, then expression (145) gives a lower bound on the probability of goal achievement. In general, for a plan with n actions such that $t_{A_1} \leq t_{A_2} \leq \ldots \leq t_{A_n}$ we have that

$$P_{now}(G \mid \wedge_{i=1}^{n} TATT(A_i, t_{A_i})) \geq P_{now}(G \mid \wedge_{i=1}^{n} ATT(A_i, t_{A_i})) \cdot \tag{146}$$
$$\prod_{i=1}^{n} P_{now}(FEAS(A_i, t_{A_i}) \mid \wedge_{j<i} ATT(A_j, t_{A_j})),$$

For example, suppose that $t_{A_1} < t_{A_2} = t_{A_3}$ then

$$P_{now}(G \mid TATT(A_1, t_{A_1}) \wedge TATT(A_2, t_{A_2}) \wedge TATT(A_3, t_{A_3})) =$$
$$P_{now}(G \mid ATT(A_1, t_{A_1}) \wedge ATT(A_2, t_{A_2}) \wedge ATT(A_3, t_{A_3})) \cdot$$
$$P_{now}(FEAS(A_3, t_{A_3}) \mid ATT(A_1, t_{A_1}) \wedge ATT(A_2, t_{A_2})) \cdot$$
$$P_{now}(FEAS(A_2, t_{A_2}) \mid ATT(A_1, t_{A_1})) \cdot$$
$$P_{now}(FEAS(A_1, t_{A_1}))$$

Now suppose that we are interested in the chance of achieving the goal through the occurrence of the plan. Then we may take G to be $G' \wedge OCC(A_1, t_{A_1}, t'_{A_1}) \wedge OCC(A_2, t_{A_2}, t'_{A_2})$, i.e., the conjunction of some goal and the occurrence of the plan. Now since $OCC(A_i, t_{A_i}, t'_{A_i})$ and $\neg ATT(A_i, t_{A_i})$ are logically incompatible, the second, third, and fourth terms in (142) are zero. Hence expression (146) represents precisely the probability that the plan achieves the goal through its occurrence:

$$P_{now}(G' \wedge OCC(A_1, t_{A_1}, t'_{A_1}) \wedge OCC(A_2, t_{A_2}, t'_{A_2}) \mid \tag{147}$$
$$TATT(A_1, t_{A_1}) \wedge TATT(A_2, t_{A_2})) =$$
$$P_{now}(G' \wedge OCC(A_1, t_{A_1}, t'_{A_1}) \wedge OCC(A_2, t_{A_2}, t'_{A_2}) \mid$$
$$ATT(A_1, t_{A_1}) \wedge ATT(A_2, t_{A_2})) \cdot$$
$$P_{now}(FEAS(A_2, t_{A_2}) \mid ATT(A_1, t_{A_1})) \cdot P_{now}(FEAS(A_1, t_{A_1}))$$

And in general,

$$P_{now}(G' \wedge_i OCC(A_i, t_{A_i}, t'_{A_i}) \mid \wedge_i TATT(A_i, t_{A_i})) = \tag{148}$$
$$P_{now}(G' \wedge_i OCC(A_i, t_{A_i}, t'_{A_i}) \mid \wedge_i ATT(A_i, t_{A_i})) \cdot$$
$$\prod_{i=1}^{n} P_{now}(FEAS(A_i, t_{A_i}) \mid \wedge_{j<i} ATT(A_j, t_{A_j}))$$

References

1. J.F. Allen. Towards a general theory of action and time. *Artificial Intelligence*, 23(2):123–154, 1984.

2. J.F. Allen. Temporal reasoning and planning. In *Reasoning About Plans*, chapter 1, pages 1–68. Morgan Kaufmann, San Mateo, CA, 1991.

3. J.F. Allen and J.A. Koomen. Planning using a temporal world model. In *Proceedings of the eighth International Joint Conference on Artificial Intelligence*, pages 741–747, Karlsruhe, W. Germany, August 1983.

4. F. Bacchus. *Representing and Reasoning With Probabilistic Knowledge*. PhD thesis, University of Alberta, 1988.

5. F. Bacchus. *Representing and Reasoning With Probabilistic Knowledge*. MIT Press, Cambridge, Mass, 1990.

6. K.R. Baker. *Introduction to Sequencing and Scheduling*. John Wiley & Sons, New York, 1974.

7. L. Chrisman. Abstract probabilistic modeling of action. In *Proceedings of the First International Conference on Artificial Intelligence Planning Systems*, pages 28–36, June 1992.

8. T. Dean, L. Pack Kaelbling, J. Kirman, and A. Nicholson. Planning with deadlines in stochastic domains. In *Proceedings of the Eleventh National Conference on Artificial Intelligence*, pages 574–579, July 1993.

9. T. Dean and K. Kanazawa. A model for reasoning about persistence and causation. *Computational Intelligence*, 5(3):142–150, 1989.

10. T. Dean and K. Kanazawa. Persistence and probabilistic projection. *IEEE Transactions on Systems, Man, and Cybernetics*, 19(3):574–585, May 1989.

11. T. Dean and Keiji Kanazawa. Probabilistic temporal reasoning. In *Proceedings of the Seventh National Conference on Artificial Intelligence*, pages 524–528, St.Paul,MN, 1988.

12. T.L. Dean and M.P. Wellman. *Planning and Control*. Morgan Kaufmann, San Mateo, CA, 1991.

13. M. Drummond and J. Bresina. Anytime synthetic projection: Maximizing the probability of goal satisfaction. In *Proceedings of the Eighth National Conference on Artificial Intelligence*, pages 138–144, Boston, MA, July 1990.

14. M. Dummett. Reply to D.H. Mellor. In B.M. Taylor, editor, *Michael Dummett*, pages 287–298. Martinus Nijhoff Publishers. Dordrecht., Netherlands, 1987.

15. D. Echeverry. *Factors for Generating Initial Construction Schedules*. PhD thesis, Dept. of Civil Engineering, University of Illinois, April 1991.

16. R. Fagin, J.Y. Halpern, and N. Megiddo. A logic for reasoning about probabilities. Technical Report RJ 6190 (60900), IBM Almaden Reasearch Center, April 1988. (also to appear in *Information and Computation*).

17. J.A. Feldman and R.F. Sproull. Decision theory and artificial intelligence II: The hungry monkey. *Artificial Intelligence*, 1:158–192, 1977.

18. R.E. Fikes and N.J. Nilsson. Strips: a new approach to the application of theorem proving to problem solving. *Artificial Intelligence*, 2:189–208, 1971.

19. P.C. Fishburn. Subjective expected utility: A review of normative theories. *Theory and Decision*, 13:129–199, 1981.

20. A.M. Frisch and P. Haddawy. Anytime deduction for probabilistic logic. *Artificial Intelligence*, 1994. (to appear).

21. A.I. Goldman. *A Theory of Human Action*. Prentice Hall, Englewood Cliffs, New Jersey, 1970.

22. A.R. Haas. Possible events, actual events, and robots. *Computational Intelligence*, 1:59–70, 1985.

23. P. Haddawy and A.M. Frisch. Convergent deduction for probabilistic logic. In *Proceedings of the Third Workshop on Uncertainty in Artificial Intelligence*, pages 278–286, Seattle, Washington, July 1987.

24. P. Haddawy and A.M. Frisch. Modal logics of higher-order probability. In R. Shachter, T.S. Levitt, J. Lemmer, and L.N. Kanal, editors, *Uncertainty in Artificial Intelligence 4*, pages 133–148. Elsevier Science Publishers, Amsterdam, 1990.

25. P. Haddawy and S. Hanks. Representations for decision-theoretic planning: Utility functions for deadline goals. In B. Nebel, C. Rich, and W. Swartout, editors, *Principles of Knowledge Representation and Reasoning: Proceedings of the Third International Conference (KR92)*, pages 71–82. Morgan Kaufmann, San Mateo, CA, 1992.

26. P. Haddawy and S. Hanks. Utility models for goal-directed decision-theoretic planners. Technical Report 93-06-04, Department of Computer Science and Engineering, University of Washington, June 1993.

27. J.Y. Halpern. An analysis of first-order logics of probability. *Artificial Intelligence*, 46:311–350, 1991.

28. J.Y. Halpern and M.R. Tuttle. Knowledge, probability, and adversaries. In *Proceedings of the Eighth Annual ACM Symposium on Principles of Distributed Computing*, pages 103–118, August 1989.

29. S. Hanks. Representing and computing temporally scoped beliefs. In *Proceedings of the Seventh National Conference on Artificial Intelligence*, pages 501–505, St.Paul,Minn, 1988.

30. S. Hanks. Practical temporal projection. In *Proceedings of the Eighth National Conference on Artificial Intelligence*, pages 158–163, Boston, July 1990.

31. S. Hanks. *Projecting Plans for Uncertain Worlds*. PhD thesis, Yale University, January 1990.

32. S. Hart and M. Shair. Probabilistic temporal logics for finite and bounded models. In *Proceedings of the Sixteenth ACM Symposium on the Theory of Computing*, pages 1–13, 1984.

33. R.M. Hogarth. Cognitive processes and the assessment of subjective probability distributions. *Journal of the American Statistical Association*, 70:271–294, 1975.

34. G.E. Hughes and M.J. Cressewell. *An Introduction to Modal Logic*. Methuen and Co., London, 1968.

35. R.C. Jeffrey. *The Logic of Decision*. McGraw-Hill, 1965.

36. K. Kanazawa. *Probability, Time, and Action*. PhD thesis, Brown University, forthcoming.

37. K. Kanazawa. A logic and time nets for probabilistic inference. In *Proceedings of the Ninth National Conference on Artificial Intelligence*, pages 360–365, July 1991.

38. R.L. Keeney and H. Raiffa. *Decisions with Multiple Objectives: Preferences and Value Tradeoffs*. Wiley, New York, 1976.

39. A. Kolmogorov. *Foundations of the Theory of Probability*. Chelsea Publishing Co., New York, 1950.

40. S. Kripke. Semantical considerations on modal logic. *Acta Philosophica Fennica*, 16:83–94, 1963. (Proceedings of a Colloquium on Modal and Many-Valued Logics, Helsinki, 23-26 Aug, 1962).

41. N. Kushmerick, S. Hanks, and D. Weld. An algorithm for probabilistic planning. Technical Report 93-06-03, Dept. of Computer Science and Engineering, University of Washington, June 1993.

42. D. Lehmann and S. Shelah. Reasoning with time and chance. *Information and Control*, 53:165–198, 1982.

43. D. Lewis. A subjectivist's guide to objective chance. In W. Harper, R. Stalnaker, and G. Pearce, editors, *Ifs*, pages 267–298. D. Reidel, Dordrecht, 1980.

44. D. Lewis. Causal decision theory. *Australasian Journal of Philosophy*, 56(1):5–30, March 1981.

45. P. Maher. Causality in the logic of decision. *Theory and Decision*, 22:155–172, 1987.

46. P. Maher. *Betting on Theories*. Cambridge University Press, 1993.

47. N.G. Martin and J.F. Allen. A language for planning with statistics. In *Proceedings of the Seventh Conference on Uncertainty in Artificial Intelligence*, pages 220–227, July 1991.

48. D. McAllester and D. Rosenblitt. Systematic nonlinear planning. In *Proceedings of the Ninth National Conference on Artificial Intelligence*, pages 634–639, 1991.

49. J. McCarthy and P. Hayes. Some philosophical problems from the standpoint of artificial intelligence. In B. Meltzer and D. Michie, editors, *Machine Intelligence 4*, pages 463–502. Edinburgh University Press, Edinburgh, UK, 1969.

50. D.V. McDermott. A temporal logic for reasoning about processes and plans. *Cognitive Science*, 6:101–155, 1982.

51. D.H. Mellor. Fixed past, unfixed future. In B.M. Taylor, editor, *Michael Dummett*, pages 166–186. Martinus Nijhoff Publishers. Dordrecht., Netherlands, 1987.

52. R.N. Pelavin. *A Formal Logic for Planning with Concurrent Actions and External Events*. PhD thesis, Univ. of Rochester, Dept. of Computer Science, 1988.

53. R.N. Pelavin. Planning with simultaneous actions and external events. In *Reasoning About Plans*, chapter 3, pages 128–211. Morgan Kaufmann, San Mateo, CA, 1991.

54. R.N. Pelavin and J.F. Allen. A formal logic of plans in temporally rich domains. *Proceedings of the IEEE*, 74(10):1364–1382, October 1986.

55. H. Raiffa. *Decision Analysis*. Addison-Wesley, Reading,MA, 1968.

56. F.P. Ramsey. Truth and probability. In D.H. Mellor, editor, *Foundations*, chapter 3, pages 58–100. Humanities Press, Atlantic Highlands, N.J., 1926. (Collection published 1978).

57. E.D. Sacerdoti. A structure for plans and behavior. Technical Note 109, SRI, August 1975.

58. L.J. Savage. *The Foundations of Statistics*. John Wiley & Sons, New York, 1954. (Second revised edition published 1972).

59. L.J. Savage. Elicitation of personal probabilities and expectations. *Journal of the American Statistical Association*, 66:783–801, 1971.

60. J.R. Shoenfield. *Mathematical Logic*. Addison-Wesley, Reading, Mass, 1967.

61. Y. Shoham. *Reasoning About Change*. MIT Press, Cambridge, MA, 1987.

62. Y. Shoham. Time for action: On the relationship between time, knowledge, and action. In *Proceedings of the Eleventh International Joint Conference on Artificial Intelligence*, pages 954–959, Detroit, August 1989.

63. B. Skyrms. *Causal Necessity*. Yale Univ. Press, New Haven, 1980.

64. B. Skyrms. Higher order degrees of belief. In D.H. Mellor, editor, *Prospects for Pragmatism*, chapter 6, pages 109–137. Cambridge Univ. Press, Cambridge, 1980.

65. J.H. Sobel. Circumstances and dominance in a causal decision theory. *Synthese*, 63:167–202, 1985.

66. P. Suppes. *A Probabilistic Theory of Causality*. Acta Philosophica Fennica, Fasc. XXIV. North-Holland, Amsterdam, 1970.

67. G.J. Sussman. *A Computer Model of Skill Acquisition*. American Elsevier, New York, 1975.
68. B.C. van Fraassen. A temporal framework for conditionals and chance. In W. Harper, R. Stalnaker, and G. Pearce, editors, *Ifs*, pages 323–340. D. Reidel, Dordrecht, 1980.
69. J. Venn. *The Logic of Chance*. MacMillan, London, 1866. (new paperback edition, Chelsea, 1962).
70. R. von Mises. *Probability, Statistics and Truth*. Allen and Unwin, London, 1957.
71. D. von Winterfeldt and W. Edwards. *Decision Analysis and Behavioral Research*. Cambridge University Press, Cambridge, 1986.
72. M. Wellman and J. Doyle. Preferential semantics for goals. In *Proceedings of the Ninth National Conference on Artificial Intelligence*, pages 698–703, Los Angeles, CA, July 1991.
73. M.P. Wellman. *Formulation of Tradeoffs in Planning Under Uncertainty*. PhD thesis, MIT, August 1988.
74. M.P. Wellman. *Formulation of Tradeoffs in Planning Under Uncertainty*. Pitman, London,UK, 1990.
75. M.P. Wellman. Qualitative probabilistic networks for planning under uncertainty. In G. Shafer and J. Pearl, editors, *Readings in Uncertain Reasoning*, chapter 9, pages 711–722. Morgan Kaufmann, San Mateo, CA, 1990.
76. M.P. Wellman. The STRIPS assumption for planning under uncertainty. In *Proceedings of the Eighth National Conference on Artificial Intelligence*, pages 198–203, July 1990.
77. M.P. Wellman and J. Doyle. Modular utility representation for decision-theoretic planning. In *Proceedings of the First International Conference on Artificial Intelligence Planning Systems*, pages 236–242, June 1992.
78. A.N. Whitehead and B.A.W. Russell. *Principia Mathematica*. Cambridge University Press, Cambridge, UK, 1910.
79. J.D. Wiest and F.K. Levy. *A Management Guide to PERT/CPM*. Prentice-Hall, Englewood Cliffs, NJ, 1969.

Springer-Verlag
and the Environment

We at Springer-Verlag firmly believe that an international science publisher has a special obligation to the environment, and our corporate policies consistently reflect this conviction.

We also expect our business partners – paper mills, printers, packaging manufacturers, etc. – to commit themselves to using environmentally friendly materials and production processes.

The paper in this book is made from low- or no-chlorine pulp and is acid free, in conformance with international standards for paper permanency.

Printing: Weihert-Druck GmbH, Darmstadt
Binding: Buchbinderei Schäffer, Grünstadt

Lecture Notes in Artificial Intelligence (LNAI)

Lecture Notes in Computer Science